Requirements for an MDM Solution

A proven approach for how to gather, document, and manage requirements for a Master Data Management solution from Inception through Implementation

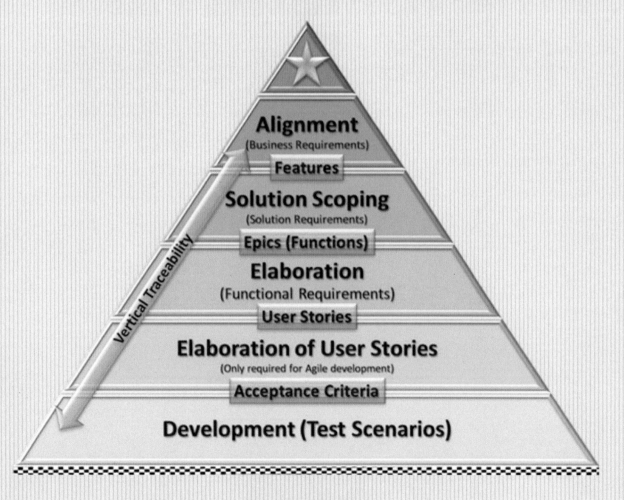

by Vicki McCracken

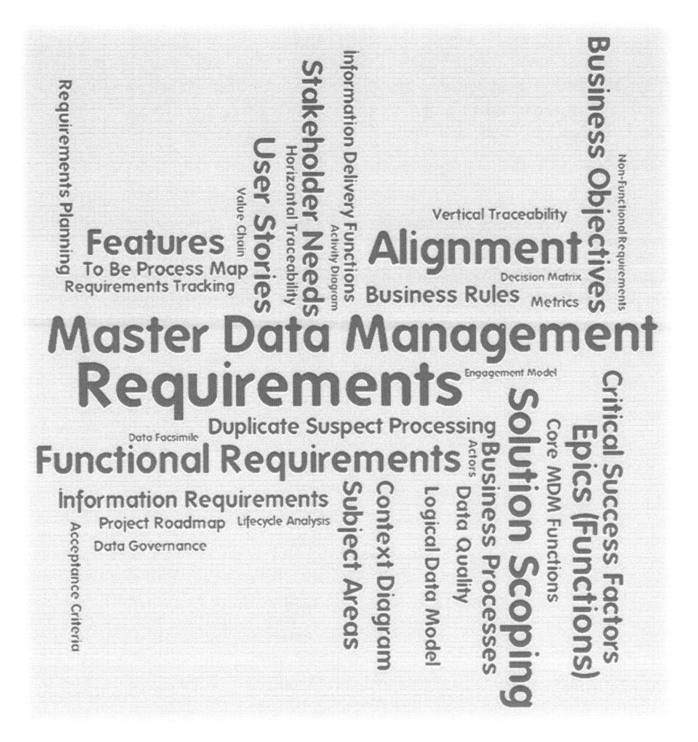

ISBN: 1533555176
ISBN-13: 978-1533555175

Printed in the United States of America

Table of Contents

List of Illustrations / Examples

Preface

The focus of this guide is to highlight a proven approach for requirements gathering and documentation for Master Data Management solutions. This includes the activities performed, the sequence of the activities, and the work products produced. Some activities are emphasized, such as the data oriented activities, where visualizations are used to ensure a consistent understanding of the requirements. In addition, the guide highlights certain activities that are unique to MDM solutions, such as Duplicate Suspect Processing. Requirements gathering and documentation activities are similar, regardless of the type of solution. What differs is the approach, the sequence and emphasis of specific activities, and the content of the work products. MDM projects do not come along often; this guide can serve as a roadmap for how to approach requirements for an MDM solution.

The guide begins with a brief overview of Master Data Management. The guide then steps through the requirements activities and work products for each Solution Development Lifecycle phase. Each work product must have a purpose and add value to upstream and/or downstream consumers. The requirements work products are described, along with an example of each work product:

- Alignment [Business Requirements - *A consensus of what is to be achieved*]:
    - Problem / Opportunity Statement
    - Business Objectives
    - Business Context Diagram and System Context Diagram
    - Conceptual Data Model, identifying Subject Areas and their relationships
    - Business Processes
    - Stakeholder Needs
    - Features
    - Critical Success Factors
- Solution Scoping [Solution Requirements - *A blueprint or foundation for the solution*]:
    - Information Requirements
    - Information Requirements visualizations, including Logical Data Model and Facsimiles
    - Elaboration of Business Processes, including To Be Process Maps
    - Data Quality, Duplicate Suspect Processing, and Functional Business Rules
    - Entity Lifecycle Analysis (State Modeling)
    - Identification of Epics (Functions)
        - Core MDM Epics (Functions)
        - Information Delivery Epics (Functions)
        - Data Quality Epics (Functions)
    - Operational and Data Quality Metrics
    - Non-Functional Requirements, including Capacity Requirements
- Elaboration [Functional Requirements for Epics (Functions) - *Specifications for development*]:
    - Epic (Function) Information Requirements, including Inputs, Outputs, and Data Updates
    - Identification and elaboration of the Business Rules the Epic (Function) must enforce
    - Activity Diagram depicting high level logical flow for the Epic (Function)
    - Identification of User Stories for the Epic (Function)
- Elaboration of User Stories, including Acceptance Criteria

Keys to success are identified for the various phases of the Solution Development Lifecycle. In addition, for Solution Scoping, there is a section which focuses on how to approach, plan, and track Solution Scoping. Finally, there is an overview of Change Management and Traceability.

Introduction

This document serves as a guide for requirements analysts on how to approach requirements for MDM development efforts. The processes and practices included in this guide are the result of developing requirements for multiple new MDM solutions, in several organizations, for different data domains, over many years. They have evolved over time, with each implementation. While the guide supports a new MDM solution implementation, the processes and practices can also be applied to enhancement efforts. For enhancement efforts, it may only be necessary to produce a subset of the work products. The guide will also support either agile development or traditional development. The difference is that for agile development, User Stories must be elaborated on; whereas for traditional development, the development can be based off of the functional requirements for the Epics (Functions). Even with traditional development, an iterative or incremental development approach should be leveraged.

The example work products included in this guide are intended for illustration purposes only. These examples contain representative data for a customer MDM solution for the Financial Services industry. The customer domain was selected, as it is a domain that is familiar to everyone; however, the approach is the same regardless of data domain. The examples have been kept simple for illustration purposes and do not represent a complete or actual MDM solution. The examples are consistent and depict how the artifacts and work products tie together. In addition, the examples may trigger a thought process or contain a topic for consideration. The Requirements Catalog work product examples are shown in an Excel format; however, if a requirements management tool is available, the work product artifacts could also be stored in the requirements management tool. The work product examples may only be excerpts for the given work product and for the Requirements Catalog work products only one line for a given row may be shown in the examples. The intent is to provide a visual representation of the work product that is being discussed, not a complete work product.

The guide assumes some familiarity with requirements gathering techniques and work products; it does not focus on techniques. This guide demonstrates how to structure the various requirements activities, to successfully gather and document requirements for an MDM solution. There are other publications that focus on techniques. BABOK (Business Analysis Book of Knowledge) has considerable details on requirements elicitation, analysis, and documentation techniques. The guide also does not focus on formulating an MDM Business Case, MDM Architecture, or technical system requirements. For more information on these topics, refer to suggested reading.

Multiple Software Vendors offer MDM software systems: IBM, Informatica, SAP, Oracle, etc. Whether a Software Vendor has been chosen, the requirements are going to drive the software selection process, or the MDM solution is going to be developed in-house; the requirements approach is the same. Requirements should be agnostic of any software system and focus on **what** capabilities the solution must provide and **not how** these capabilities will be implemented. For software selection efforts, it is important to complete both Alignment [Business Requirements] and Solution Scoping [Solution Requirements], prior to proceeding with the software selection process.

Requirements work products add value to both upstream and downstream consumers by:

- Providing stakeholders a clear, concise, and thorough description of the proposed MDM solution
- Serving as a blueprint for the development and testing teams to build the MDM solution
- Becoming the systems documentation for the eventual MDM solution, after implementation

Good requirements are the cornerstone of every project, ensuring the project has a strong foundation. Design, Development, and Testing are also important; however, a strong requirements foundation, along with a structure to ensure traceability, is essential for a successful project.

MDM Overview

Master Data Management Overview

A Master Data Management solution brings together business critical information that is distributed across multiple Core Processing systems in an organization into a single, consolidated, authoritative, trusted view. This view is often referred to as the "golden record" and seeks to provide a single version of the truth. Because of the fact that the solution is housing the "golden record", there is usually a Data Steward assigned to monitor and manage the data.

The MDM solution consists of an operational data store, along with services to allow the information to be accessed and maintained by Front End Application systems. Information may also be shared with Information Delivery systems. Typical domains for Master Data Management Solutions include:

- Customer
- Supplier
- Provider
- Product

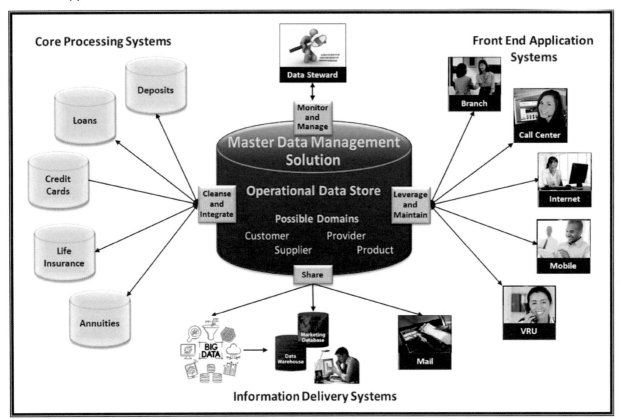

Figure 1: Master Data Management Solution Overview

For more information on Master Data Management and MDM architecture, refer to suggested reading.

How does an MDM solution differ from a Data Warehouse solution

A Master Data Management solution is operational, where Front End Application systems interact with the MDM Solution to access and **update** information. A Data Warehouse solution is analytical and represents a historical view of the data. Integration occurs behind the scenes with a Data Warehouse system. An MDM solution may feed a Data Warehouse system.

Alignment – Business Requirements

The first step in defining the requirements for an MDM solution is to gain alignment on the Business Requirements (**what** is to be achieved). This phase is also referred to as the Initiate phase or Inception phase. This guide focuses on the functional alignment activities; however, at the same time, technical alignment should occur for the conceptual architecture. The functional alignment activities are similar to other types of solutions, with the exception that more emphasis is placed on data, by identifying Subject Areas and creating a Conceptual Data Model. A good approach for alignment is to:

- Interview the project sponsors and key stakeholders to elicit the Business Requirements
- Consolidate the information from the interviews into a PowerPoint presentation
- Conduct facilitated session(s) to review, adjust, and gain consensus from all stakeholders

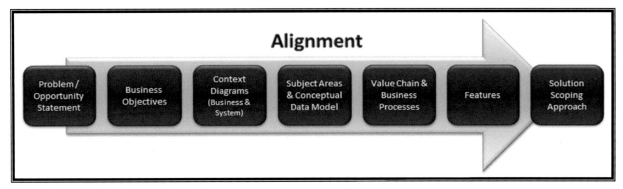

Figure 2: Functional Alignment [Business Requirements] Activities

Define the Problem / Opportunity Statement

Document the problem that is to be solved with the MDM solution. Below are some common problems that MDM solutions solve:

- Lack of enterprise view of the data, resulting in less effective servicing and cross selling
- Inconsistent customer experience across delivery channels as a result of duplicate data and services, where a customer may see different information depending on the delivery channel
- Operational inefficiencies, where the same data update needs to be made in multiple systems
- Inconsistent data (i.e., different terminology or names, different values, different formats, etc.), when data is distributed across multiple systems, resulting in confusion and misinterpretation of the information

Capture Business Objectives

Document what the project sponsors are expecting to accomplish with the MDM solution; **why** are the project sponsors undertaking this effort. Some typical Business Objectives for MDM solutions include:

- Create a single, consolidated, enterprise view (golden record) of the customer, that will provide the basis for more effective servicing and cross selling
- Gain operational efficiencies, by reducing duplicate input of data
- Improve data quality and data inconsistencies, thereby improving the customer experience
- Provide a consistent experience for consumers across delivery channels
- Improve customer experience, ensuring that when data is updated, it is updated everywhere
- Deliver the MDM solution incrementally, to achieve benefits earlier
- Simplify ongoing integration and new application development

Along with the Business Objectives, also capture the benefits or what success looks like.

Define the Context of the MDM solution

Understand who and what will be interacting with the MDM solution. The Business Context diagram will identify both business areas that add and maintain the information and also the business areas that will benefit from the information. The System Context diagram will identify:

- Core Processing systems that will source the information
- Front End Application systems that will interact with the MDM solution
- Information Delivery Systems that will receive information from the MDM solution

The context diagrams establish the preliminary actor catalog.

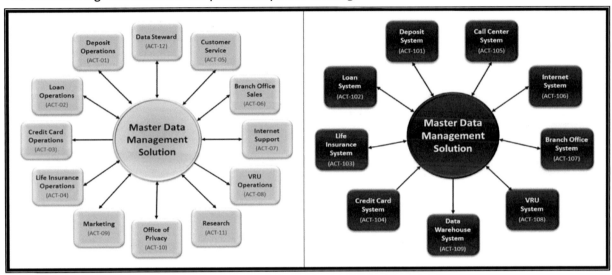

Figure 3: Example of Business Context diagram (left) and System Context diagram (right)

Identify the Subject Areas Involved

Define the extent of the information the stakeholders envision being stored in the MDM solution. The Subject Areas should be defined in business terms and can be represented visually in the form of a Conceptual Data Model. These subject areas are the basis for the Information Requirements catalog.

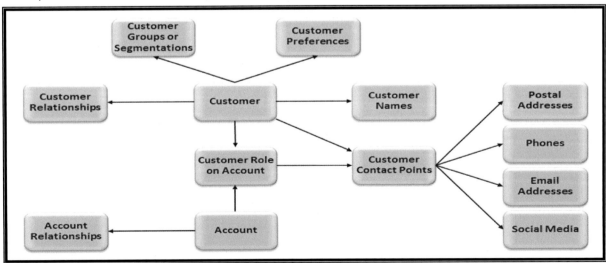

Figure 4: Example of Conceptual Data Model

Identify the Business Processes Involved

Analyze the Front End Application systems to identify what Business Processes they are performing on the MDM data. Also analyze the Value Chain for the domain to identify applicable Business Processes. These business processes will be the basis for the Business Processes catalog.

Figure 5: Example of Value Chain with applicable Business Processes

A matrix can help gain a better understanding of the Actors, along with the business processes and subject areas the Actors are related to. This matrix will provide value during Solution Scoping.

		Business Processes										Subject Areas							
		BP-01	BP-02	BP-03	BP-04	BP-05	BP-06	BP-07	BP-08	BP-09	BP-13	IR-01	IR-02	IR-03	IR-04	IR-05	IR-06	IR-07	IR-09
		Source Accounts	Search and View Account	Search and View Customer	Modify Customer Information	Open Account	Modify Account Information	Register User	Login User	Forgot Username	Acquire Prospects	Customer Profile Information	Customer Contact Point Information	Account Summary	Account to Account Relationship	Customer Role on Account	Customer to Customer Relationship	Customer Grouping	Customer Preference
Human Actors	ACT-01 Deposit Operations		X	X	X	X	X					R, C, U	R, C, U	R, C, U	R, C, U	R, C, U			R, C, U
	ACT-02 Loan Operations		X	X	X	X	X					R, C, U	R, C, U	R, C, U	R, C, U	R, C, U			R, C, U
	ACT-03 Credit Card Operations		X	X	X	X	X					R, C, U	R, C, U	R, C, U	R, C, U	R, C, U			R, C, U
	ACT-04 Life Insurance Operations		X	X	X	X	X					R, C, U	R, C, U	R, C, U	R, C, U	R, C, U			R, C, U
	ACT-05 Customer Service		X	X	X	X	X					R, C, U	R, C, U	R, C, U	R, C, U	R, C, U	R, C, U		R, C, U
	ACT-06 Branch Office Sales		X	X	X	X	X				X	R, C, U	R, C, U	R, C, U	R, C, U	R, C, U	R, C, U	R, C, U	R, C, U
	ACT-07 Internet Support		X	X	X	X	X	X	X	X	X	R, U	R, U	R	R	R	R	R	R
	ACT-12 Data Steward		X	X	X							R, U	R, U	R	R, C, U	R	R, C, U	R	R
	ACT-13 Customer							X	X	X		R, U	R, U	R	R, C, U	R	R, C, U		R, C, U
System Actors	ACT-101 Deposit System	X	X			X	X					R, C, U	R, C, U	C, U	R, C, U	R, C, U			R, C, U
	ACT-102 Loan System	X	X			X						R, C, U	R, C, U	C, U	R, C, U	R, C, U			R, C, U
	ACT-103 Life Insurance System	X				X						C, U	C, U	C, U	C, U	C, U			C, U
	ACT-104 Credit Card System	X				X						C, U	C, U	C, U	C, U	C, U			C, U
	ACT-105 Call Center System		X	X	X	X	X					R, C, U	R, C, U	R, C, U	R, C, U	R, C, U	R, C, U	R, C, U	R, C, U
	ACT-106 Internet System		X	X	X	X	X	X	X	X	X	R, C, U	R, C, U	R, C, U	R, C, U	R, C, U	R, C, U	R	R, C, U
	ACT-109 Data Warehouse System											R	R	R	R	R	R	R	R

Figure 6: Example of Actor to Business Processes / Subject Areas Matrix

Identify the Stakeholder Needs

Elicit the Stakeholder Needs. Stakeholder Needs are more specific than the business objectives and may be specific to a particular business area. Each Stakeholder Need should trace to a Business Objective. If it does not, either there is a missing business objective or the stakeholder need is not valid. For each Stakeholder Need, identify the Stakeholders for which it is a requirement. Examples may include:

- Provide a comprehensive, consistent, and consolidated cross-channel view of the customer
- Improve data and search accuracy by providing standardized Customer Information
- Eliminate duplicate data entry
- Enable the ability to make real-time updates
- Gain consensus on and document terminology, data definitions, and data values
- Define and adhere to visibility or data security rules
- Enable tracing of the date information was modified and which system/user provided the update
- The MDM solution must be available and high performing

Define the Features

Define the features or solution characteristics. These will come from the business objectives, stakeholder needs, subject areas, business processes, and context diagrams. Each feature must trace to at least one business objective and at least one stakeholder need. If it does not, either there is a missing business objective / stakeholder need or the feature is not valid. In addition, each business objective / stakeholder need must trace to at least one feature. If not, there is a feature missing.

Features

- A comprehensive, consistent, and consolidated cross-channel view of a Customer, including:
  - Customer Profile Information
  - Customer Contact Point Information
  - Account Summary
  - Account to Account Relationship
  - Customer Role on Account
  - Customer to Customer Relationship
  - Customer Grouping
  - Customer Segmentation
  - Customer Preference
- Processes to Load, Establish, Modify, Search, and View Customer Information
- Processes to Load, Establish, Modify, Search, and View Account Information
- Process to Notify systems of Customer and Account updates
- Process to Collapse multiple Customers into one
- Make Customer Information available in standard formats (i.e., extracts, views)
- Provide the following capabilities when Establishing or Modifying Information:
  - Enable customer matching as part of Establish Customer process
  - Enforce data survivorship rules as part of Establish Customer process
  - Standardize all addresses when Establishing or Modifying Customer Information
  - Ensure Data Quality when Establishing or Modifying Customer Information
  - Support Customer Lifecycles (i.e., Current, Prospective, Former, …)
  - Track the date the data was modified or added and which system / user provided the update
- Source Account Information from the following Core Processing Systems:
  - Deposits System
  - Loans System
  - Credit Cards System
  - Life Insurance System
- Integrate the following Front End Application Systems:
  - Call Center System
  - Branch Office System
  - Internet System
  - VRU System
- Ensure sensitive Customer information is properly secured (Visibility)
- Provide mechanism (i.e., statistics, reports, dashboard) – to monitor quality of the data
- Ensure solution is scalable
- Provide a mechanism to track who has viewed Customer and Account Information

---

Figure 7: Example of Solution Features

The features should be prioritized and can optionally be grouped into work packages.

Out of Scope items should also be called out. These are items that individuals may think are part of scope; however, for some reason have been deemed out of scope. When documenting the Out of Scope items, include the reasons for the items being out of scope.

Identify Critical Success Factors

Identify the Critical Success Factors for the project. If addressed properly, these factors will significantly improve the chances of success. Some common Critical Success Factors for MDM solutions are:

- Executive Management and Stakeholder Commitment and Support
- Organizational Change Management: Ensuring the organization has an understanding of the purpose, benefit, and impact of the MDM solution, and embraces the "golden record" concept
- Availability of Business Subject Matter Experts
- Availability of Technical Resources with appropriate MDM experience
- Data Governance participation to gain consensus on data definitions and data quality rules
- Commitment to establish a Data Stewardship group to monitor and manage the MDM database
- Incremental Implementation Approach to deliver value incrementally over time
- Flexible design to efficiently support future requirements

Establish Initial Implementation Rollout Strategy (Project Roadmap)

Establish an Implementation Rollout Strategy for the MDM solution. The prioritized features or work packages and their dependencies are input into this process. It is important for the development of the MDM solution to be out in front of the sourcing efforts, and for the sourcing efforts to be out in front of the front-end systems development. To develop the Rollout Strategy, it is important to understand:

- what subject areas are the most critical
- what business processes are the most critical
- what source systems are the most critical
- what consuming application systems (front-end and information delivery) are the most critical
- what source systems and subject areas the consuming application systems are dependent on

The implementation rollout strategy should start with the functionality which provides the most value and incrementally implement the MDM solution, to allow for the benefits to begin being realized as soon as possible. The implementation and adoption of the Master Data Management solution is an evolution that will mature over time, increasing both the functionality and value of the solution, along with improving the quality of the data.

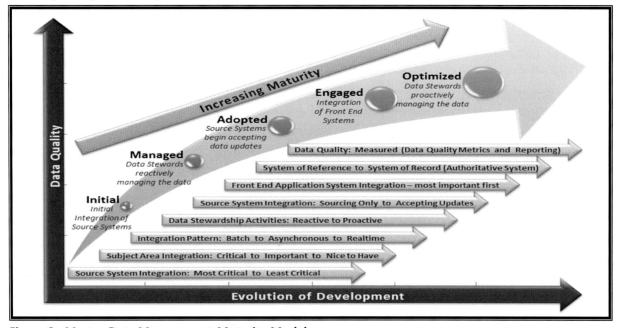

Figure 8: Master Data Management Maturity Model

Solution Scoping Approach

Solution Scoping Approach Overview

An overall Solution Scoping effort should be conducted up front that will serve as the foundation or blueprint for the MDM solution. This initial effort will cover the breadth of the MDM solution defined in the Business Requirements during Alignment, with enough depth to ensure:

- Requirements are comprehensive, based on key source systems, to minimize rework
- Stakeholders are aligned on the solution, prior to investment
- There is a clear and common understanding of the solution requirements, prior to kicking off multiple concurrent development efforts

The more complex the solution, the more extensive / deeper the initial solution scoping effort must be.

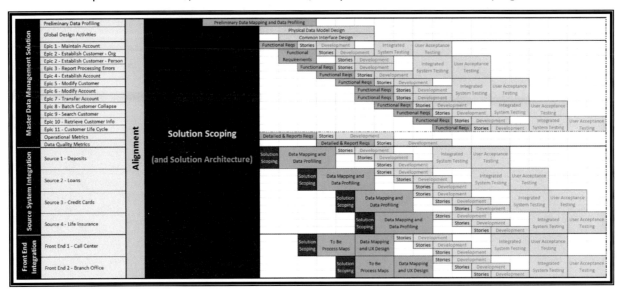

Figure 9: Requirements Approach

The initial Solution Scoping effort may take 2-4 months, depending on size, complexity, and familiarity of participants with the domain. While this may seem like a lot of time, it will save substantially more time in the long run by reducing costly rework. This is because of:

- Interdependencies between data – information from one subject area may affect the way another subject area is represented. Understanding how the subject areas relate to one another up front will avoid rework when integrating new subject areas.

- Interdependencies between systems – as a result of integrating multiple source systems with similar data and capabilities. Ensuring the information requirements, business rules, and processes are comprehensive and support all systems being integrated (or at minimal the key systems being integrated), will avoid rework when integrating a new source system.

This approach will deliver quality and comprehensive requirements that will support, not impede, the successful implementation of the MDM solution in the long run, allowing for multiple concurrent development efforts to begin after the initial Solution Scoping effort concludes.

Other types of solutions (i.e., developing a new Front-End system or implementing a new Core Processing system) may not have the same need for an overall Solution Scoping effort. For these types of solutions, Solution Scoping can be performed iteratively or incrementally.

Solution Scoping Overview

For new Data Centric efforts, it is valuable to take time up front in Solution Scoping to focus on the information requirements and data quality rules, prior to conducting business process analysis.

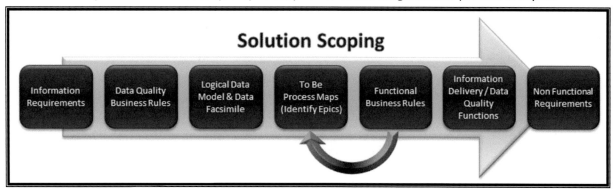

Figure 10: Solution Scoping [Solution Requirements] Activities

Solution Scoping Input [Business Requirements]

The input to the Solution Scoping phase is the output from the Alignment phase, this includes:

- Business Objectives and Stakeholder Needs
- Value Chain, including Business Processes
- Subject Areas, including Conceptual Data Model
- Context Diagrams (Business and System), including preliminary Actor Catalog
- Prioritized Features
- Out of Scope items

This information can be plotted and displayed in the team space for reference during Solution Scoping.

Solution Scoping Output [Solution Requirements]

The output from the Solution Scoping phase is a comprehensive requirements catalog, containing:

- Actors
- Business Processes, including To Be Process Maps
- Information Requirements, including Logical Data Model and Facsimiles
- Business Rules (Data Quality, Duplicate Suspect Processing, and Functional)
- Epics (Functions) - which consist of:
    - Core MDM Epics (Functions)
    - Data Quality Epics (Functions)
    - Information Delivery Epics (Functions)
- Non-Functional and Capacity Requirements

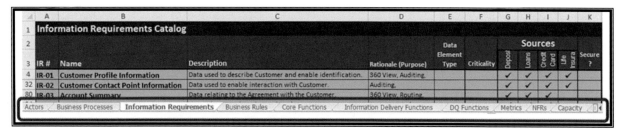

Figure 11: Example of Requirements Catalog - Contents

The Preliminary Actors, Business Processes, and Subject Areas were identified during Alignment.

Examples of the requirements catalog are provided in the Solution Scoping section of this guide, using Excel. However, a requirements management tool may be used for managing these requirements. Even with a requirements management tool, it may be beneficial to develop the Requirements Catalog in Excel and load the information into the Requirements Management tool at the end of Solution Scoping. This is because the ability to make global or mass changes may be more efficient in Excel. In addition, presentation may be easier and summary information may be cleaner in Excel.

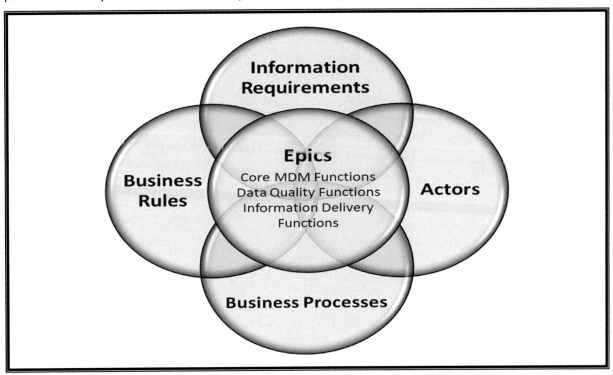

Figure 12: Solution Scoping Output [Solution Requirements]

Engagement Model

Because of the consensus required across multiple areas, facilitated sessions are a great forum to gain consensus on the requirements. The MDM solution is an enterprise application; it may not be possible to include **all** business areas in the Solution Scoping facilitated sessions. A good approach is to:

- Establish a Core Team of 4-7 individuals, consisting of Business Lead(s), Requirements Analyst(s), Architect, and Data Specialist. The Core Team is responsible for preparing a draft of the work product prior to the facilitated sessions, which will serve as a starting point for the discussion. Conduct regularly scheduled Core Team meetings to:
  - Discuss each work product and assign the individual responsible for preparing the draft
  - Review draft work products
  - Brainstorm on the approach for the extended team sessions and determine which core team member will facilitate the session. While the requirements lead may facilitate a majority of the extended team sessions; mix it up and have other Core Team members facilitate specific sessions.

  The Core Team is also responsible for working with Data Governance and the Office of Privacy to ensure they are in agreement with the solution, and all glossary terms and definitions.

- Establish an Extended Team of 15-20 individuals, consisting of both business and technical representatives that represent the key stakeholders. This extended team must have the authority to make decisions. This extended team will meet twice a week for 2 ½ to 3 hours per session to review and finalize the work products. Teleconferences, with emeetings, are a great way to engage remote participants. If conducted properly, these sessions will be collaborative, productive, and fun. The extended team is responsible for confirmation, communication, and coordination with any additional business SMEs they represent.

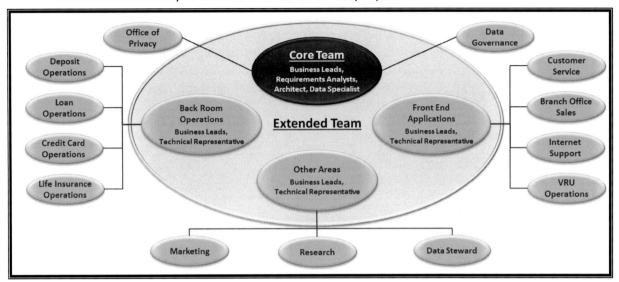

Figure 13: Example of Engagement Model

Solution Scoping Planning

To be efficient and effective, take time up front to plan out the Solution Scoping sessions. This will not only serve as the work plan for the Solution Scoping effort; it also allows the extended team to schedule specific SMEs to attend certain sessions. Based on the Business Requirements defined in Alignment, identify the Solution Scoping activities, determine the order based on dependencies, determine the effort for each activity, and create a calendar showing what activities are scheduled for each facilitated session.

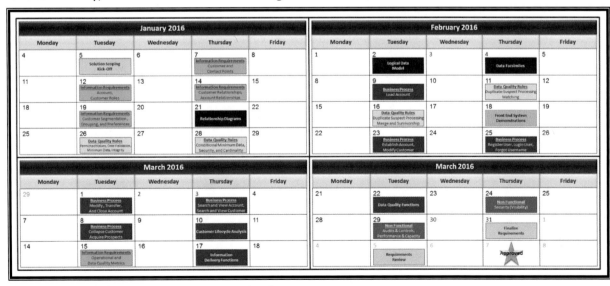

Figure 14: Example of Solution Scoping Calendar

Solution Scoping Tracking

An agile task board can be used to track the progress of the activities, with the following columns:

- Backlog - the activities that have not yet started
- Draft in Progress - identifies the activities that the Core Team is currently working on
- Draft Completed - identifies the activities where the Core Team has completed a draft
- Core Team Review - identifies the activities that are currently under review by the Core Team
- Core Team Complete - identifies the activities that are ready for the Extended Team
- Extended Team Review - identifies the activities currently being reviewed by the Extended Team
- Complete - identifies the activities where the Extended Team has finalized the work product

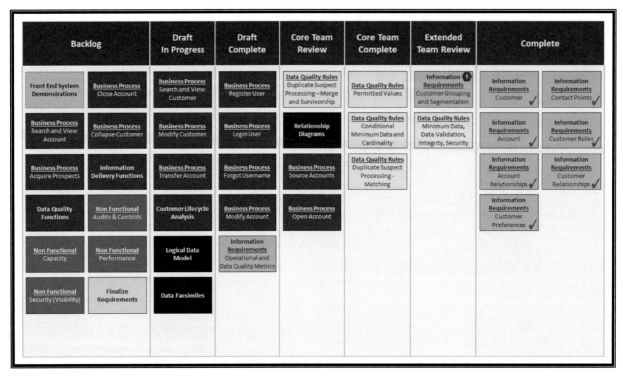

Figure 15: Example of Solution Scoping Agile Task Board (Kanban Board)

A plot of the solution scoping calendar can be displayed beside the agile board for reference. The solution scoping calendar, along with the agile task board, allows leadership and stakeholders to review current status and see if there are any roadblocks.

Solution Scoping Approach Summary

Every project is different; there is no "one size fits all". Take time after Alignment and prior to Solution Scoping to:

- Review the Business Requirements produced during Alignment
- Visualize the Solution Requirements that will be produced out of Solution Scoping
- Identify the activities and effort required to produce the Solution Requirements
- Layout a plan to accomplish those activities

This will allow Solution Scoping to proceed smoothly, and also allow the progress to be tracked, status to be accurately reported, and the Solution Scoping plan to be adjusted if necessary.

Solution Scoping – Solution Requirements

Conduct Solution Scoping Kick-Off

The first step of Solution Scoping is to have a kick-off meeting to orient the Extended Team to the project, the approach that will be followed during Solution Scoping, their participation in Solution Scoping, and the Solution Requirements that will be produced out of Solution Scoping. Similar to Alignment, the Solution Scoping process is similar to other types of solutions, with the exception that more emphasis is placed on the data activities, including Information Requirements, Data Quality business rules, and the Logical Data Model; along with a focus on the Core MDM Functions during Business Process Analysis. An Agenda for the Solution Scoping Kick-off meeting might include:

- Project Organization Structure
- Review the Business Requirements Work Products *(optional – see below)*
  - Problem / Opportunity Statement
  - Business Objectives
  - Stakeholder Needs
  - Value Chain and Business Processes
  - Subject Areas, including conceptual data model
  - Context Diagrams (Business and System)
  - Features
  - Out of Scope items
- Review the Solution Scoping Approach
  - Solution Scoping Activities
  - Solution Scoping Timeline and Calendar
  - Core Requirements Team representatives
  - Engagement Model
  - Extended Team
- Review the Solution Requirements Work Products to be produced
  - Requirements Catalog
    - Actors Catalog
    - Information Requirements Catalog
    - Business Rules Catalog
    - Business Processes Catalog
    - Epics Catalogs
      - Epics – Core MDM Functions
      - Epics – Information Delivery Functions
      - Epics – Data Quality Functions
    - Non-Functional Requirements
    - Capacity Requirements
  - Logical Data Model
  - Logical Data Facsimiles
  - To Be Process Maps
  - Consideration Analysis
- Session Expectations
- Review and Approval Process

Review of the Business Requirements Work Products is only necessary if the Extended Team was not involved in the Alignment phase.

Define Information Requirements

For data centric solutions, it is valuable to take time at the beginning of Solution Scoping to define the Information Requirements. This is because the MDM solution involves information from multiple Business Areas and Core Processing systems that may use different terminology to define the same information. It is important for the Information Requirements and definitions to be in business terms, agnostic of any system. It is also important to gain consensus on terminology and definitions from both the extended team and data governance. Record all agreed upon terms and definitions in a glossary.

Iteratively, analyze each Subject Area defined during alignment and define the individual Information Requirements for each Subject Area. This includes information required to uniquely identify an object, information required for duplicate suspect processing (matching and survivorship), and information which is to be shared across multiple consuming application systems. It should not include dynamic application data from the source systems (i.e., information which changes frequently). Organize the Information Requirements into logical groupings. In addition, for each Information Requirement, define:

- **IR #**   Unique Identifier for Information Requirement
- **Name**   The agreed upon name for the Information Requirement. The Information Requirement name should be in business terms
- **Description**   Definition for Information Requirement
- **Rationale (Purpose)**   Examples:
  - 360 View   Information that is part of the consolidated view of the customer
  - Communication   Information used to communicate with the customer
  - Auditing   Information used to track who and when data is accessed or updated
  - Identifying   Information used in identifying a customer
  - Matching   Information used by the Duplicate Suspect Matching process
  - Survivorship   used in determining what information is retained during a collapse
- **Data Element Type**   Type Code, Date, Date/Time, Identifier, Indicator, Name, Number, Text
- **Criticality**   Examples:
  - Critical   Must be part of MDM solution
  - Important   Brings substantial business value to MDM solution
  - Medium   May be important in the future or brings value to a specific business area
  - Nice   Nice to have.
- **Information Source**   Identifies the source systems of the information
- **Security Information**   Indicates whether access to the information must be restricted

Information Requirements Catalog

IR #	Name	Description	Rationale (Purpose)	Data Element Type	Criticality	Deposits	Loans	Credit Card	Life Insurance	Secure?
IR-01	Customer Profile Information	Data used to describe Customer and enable identification.	360 View, Auditing,			✓	✓	✓	✓	
IR-01-3	Customer Tax Identification	Data relating to the Tax Identification for the Customer.				✓	✓	✓	✓	
IR-01-3-1	Customer Taxpayer Identification Type	Represents the type of Taxpayer Identification Number. This	Identifying	Code	Critical	✓	✓			
IR-01-3-2	Customer Taxpayer Identification Number	Number used to identify a Customer for U.S. Tax Reporting	Identifying, Matching	Number	Critical	✓	✓	✓	✓	Mask
IR-01-3	Customer Name	Data relating to the Name(s) of the Customer.				✓	✓	✓	✓	
IR-01-4-1	Person Name	Data specific to the name for a Person.				✓	✓	✓	✓	
IR-01-4-1-01	Person Name Type Code	Represents the type of name used by a Person.	Communication	Code	Critical	✓	✓	✓	✓	
IR-01-4-1-02	Prefix Type Code	Component of a Person Name representing a title that precedes	Communication	Code	Important	✓	✓	✓		
IR-01-4-1-03	First Name	Component of a Person Name representing the first given name	Identifying,	Name	Critical	✓	✓	✓	✓	
IR-01-4-1-04	Middle Name	Component of a Person Name representing the second given	Identifying.	Name	Critical	✓	✓	✓	✓	
IR-01-4-1-05	Last Name	Component of a Person Name representing the surname or	Identifying.	Name	Critical	✓	✓	✓	✓	

Figure 16: Example of Information Requirements Catalog (Functional Data Dictionary)

In addition, each Information Requirement can be classified as either System of Record or System of Reference, or Both. Both occurs when the classification may vary depending on Source System or Type. Each Information Requirement must trace back to a feature. The information requirements catalog will be used by the MDM development effort and also leveraged by the Sourcing and Front End development efforts for data mapping.

Define Data Quality Business Rules

The next step is to define the Business Rules that ensure the data quality of the Information Requirements and defines what is acceptable data. The Business Rules must be clear, concise, thorough, testable, and agnostic of any system. Similar to the Information Requirements, it is important to gain consensus from the extended team and data governance because data quality rules, especially permitted value rules, may vary depending on Business Area and Core Processing system. Enterprise Data Quality rules must be defined for the MDM solution, which support all Business Areas. Analyze each individual Information Requirement and define the Data Quality Business Rules. This includes:

- **BR #**   Unique Identifier for Business Rule
- **BR Name**   The name for the Business Rule
- **Detailed Rule**   The complete Business Rule
- **Business Rule Type**
    - Minimum Data   defines what information is required to establish a customer
    - Conditional Minimum Data   defines what information is required to create a specific logical group of information or entity (i.e., for Person Name – first and last name are required, for Customer Address – street address, city, state, and zip are required, etc. ...)
    - Data Validation   ensures data for a given field conforms to data quality standards and is acceptable (Some ETL tools come with some basic validation rules. If applicable, evaluate these rules to see if they apply.)
    - Permitted Values   defines the agreed upon allowable values or reference data for a Type Code field
    - Data Integrity   ensures data across multiple fields is consistent
    - Data Cardinality   defines how many occurrences are allowed for a specific data element or logical group of information, and whether the information is optional (i.e., 1, 0 to 1, 0 to many, 1 to many)
- **Category** - to aid in categorizing business rules during solution scoping only. Will be replaced by traceability to Epics (Functions) and Information Requirements during functional requirements.
- **Criticality** (see Information Requirements section for definitions)
- **Behavior / Comments** – Invalid data should not be integrated into the MDM solution. The behavior may differ depending on the processing mode (i.e., batch / asynchronous (non-interactive) vs synchronous (interactive)). For example, the behavior when a business rule fails in a non-interactive mode may be to discard the failed information and continue to process the transaction; whereas in an interactive mode the behavior may be to error the transaction.

These rules may be refined during functional requirements and data profiling activities, elaborating on the behavior. In addition, System Rules and Data Transformation Rules may be added as part of functional requirements and data profiling activities.

Business Rules Catalog

BR #	BR Name	Detailed Rule	Type (Data / Functional)	Category (Subject Area / Process)	Criticality (L/M/H)	Behavior / Comments
BR-01	Customer Information Business Rules					
BR-01-11	Data Validation - Taxpayer Identification Number	A TIN must be 9 characters in length and must only be numeric digits.	Data Validation	Tax Identification	H	Return Error
BR-01-12	Data Cardinality - Taxpayer Identification Number	A Customer may have one and only one active Taxpayer Identification	Data Cardinality /	Tax Identification	H	Multiple are received on input:
BR-01-13	Permitted Values - Taxpayer Identification Number Type	TIN	Permitted Values	Taxpayer Identification Number	H	Default to TIN
BR-01-14	Data Survivorship - Customer - Taxpayer Identification	The taxpayer identification must either match or be empty to be	Data Survivorship / Data	Tax Identification	H	
BR-01-15	Visibility Restriction - Taxpayer Identification Number	Taxpayer Identification Number must be masked on all DPIM	Visibility	Tax Identification	H	Exceptions to this rule (based
BR-01-16	Data Cardinality - Customer Name	A Customer must have at least one, but could have many names.	Data Cardinality	Name	H	Return Error
BR-01-17	Data Survivorship - Customer Name	All Active Customer Names must survive to the new Customer,	Data Survivorship / Data	Name	H	If a duplicate name is received
BR-01-18	Conditional Data - Customer Person Name	For Customer Person Name - Person Name Type Code, First Name, and	Conditional Minimum Data	Person Name	H	Return Error

Figure 17: Example of Business Rules Catalog

Develop Logical Data Model / Data Facsimiles

The next step is to create visualizations to ensure the extended team is in agreement as to how the information relates together, confirming the data cardinality rules. These include:

- Relationship Diagrams (optional)
- Logical Data Model (Entity Relationship Diagram)
- Logical Data Facsimiles

These deliverables provide considerable value for any data centric solution, including MDM solutions.

If there is an area or subject areas, where there is not a clear understanding of how the information relates together, it is helpful to create a relationship diagram to gain understanding and ensure consensus. For example, if it is unclear whether the Customer Address relates to the Account or the Customer Role on an Account, a relationship diagram can be used to visualize and confirm. This diagram is an optional working document, which does not need to be baselined as an official work product.

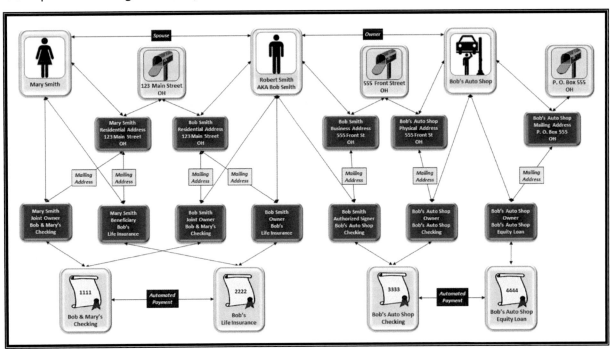

Figure 18: Example of Relationship Diagram

The next step is to create a high-level logical data model (entity relationship diagram) to depict the relationships between the subject areas / logical groupings of information requirements (entities) and the data cardinality rules (i.e., 0 to Many, 1 to Many, 0 to 1, 1 and only 1).

Finally, Logical Data Facsimiles are created that illustrate how actual data will be represented in the logical data model. It may be necessary to create multiple Logical Data Facsimiles to represent different business scenarios.

These visualizations ensure the extended team and stakeholders have a clear and common understanding of the Information Requirements and Data Cardinality rules. Depending on the organization, a Data Modeler may be responsible for producing these deliverables. Regardless of whether the Requirements Analyst or a Data Modeler is responsible for producing these deliverables, they are key deliverables in the requirements process for an MDM solution.

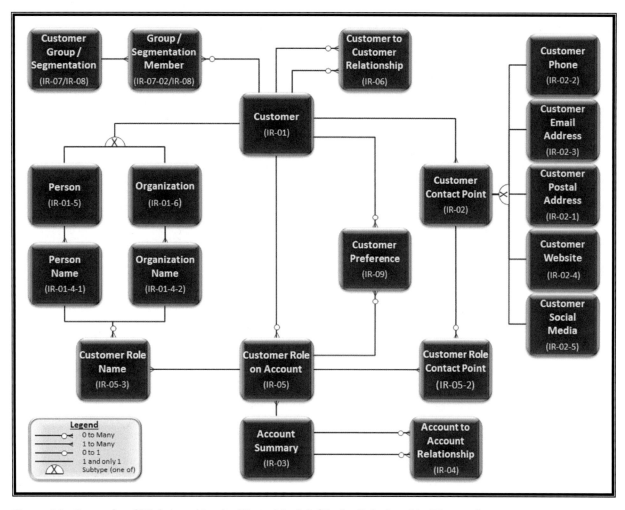

Figure 19: Example of High-Level Logical Data Model (Entity Relationship Diagram)

For more information on Data Modeling, refer to suggested reading - *"Data Modeling Made Simple"*.

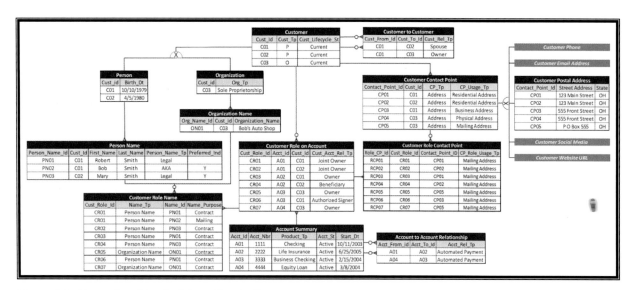

Figure 20: Example of Logical Data Facsimile

Solution Scoping – Solution Requirements - Define Duplicate Suspect Processing Rules

Define Duplicate Suspect Processing Rules

Functionality that is unique to a Master Data Management solution is integrating / consolidating similar information from multiple Core Processing or Source systems into a single Operational Data Store. In order to support this functionality, the Master Data Management solution requires rules to determine what constitutes both a duplicate occurrence for the domain of the Master Data Management solution and how to handle those duplicate records. This is known as "Duplicate Suspect Processing" (also known as "Duplicate Record Processing", "Match / Merge Processing", and "Data Deduplication").

There are three types of business rules that support Duplicate Suspect Processing:

- **Data Cleansing** or **Data Transformation** Rules
- **Data Matching** Rules
- **Data Survivorship** Rules

Data Cleansing or Data Transformation Rules ensure the data is in a consistent format prior to Duplicate Suspect Processing. Some examples include:

- Processing all addresses through address standardization or CASS certified software. This may need to include parsing supplemental address verbiage (i.e., ATTN, C/O, DBA, Internal Mail Codes, etc.) into a separate data element.

- Parsing Person Name Generational Suffix out of Last Name, First Name, or Middle Name fields into a separate data element.

- Applying a common format to Taxpayer Identification Numbers or Phone Numbers.

Data Matching Rules are rules that specify what constitutes a match or a duplicate for the MDM domain, and also what constitutes a suspect or suspected duplicate. There are two types of matching:

- Deterministic Matching - explicitly defines what constitutes a match and a suspect
- Probabilistic Matching - more of a black box solution, based on fuzzy matching logic

Both Deterministic and Probabilistic matching require the identification of Critical Data Elements that will be used to determine if two occurrences are matches, suspects, or not a match. In addition, suspects can be grouped into two categories: 1 - more likely than not to be a duplicate and 2 - more likely than not to be two distinct records. Examples of Critical Data Elements for the Customer domain are Name, Address, Taxpayer Identification Number, and Birth Date for persons.

Probabilistic Matching is where the importance or weight of each Critical Data Element is defined. Probabilistic Matching then uses fuzzy matching logic to assign a score to each Critical Data Element, based on how closely the values match. The weights, along with the scores, for all Critical Data Elements, are used to calculate the probability of the two occurrences being a match. A threshold is set to specify the probability percentage which constitutes a match or a suspect. A variety of algorithms can be used for the fuzzy matching logic (different software systems use different algorithms). Probabilistic Matching is typically used for a marketing database, where it is not essential to understand what explicitly caused the two occurrences to be identified as a duplicate.

Deterministic Matching is where the rules are explicitly defined as to what constitutes a match and a suspect. Deterministic Matching is often used when the information in the database is going to be used for operational purposes and it is critical to be able to explicitly control what is identified as a match. For example, if the MDM solution is for customer data and is used by the Internet System to display a consolidated view of the customers' accounts to the customer, it is critical to understand what is defined as a match. The following is an example of a duplicate suspect processing decision matrix for deterministic matching.

18   Requirements for an MDM Solution

TIN SSN, ITIN, ATIN	Address	Birth Date	Last Name / Suffix	First Name / Middle	Matching Data	Non-Matching Data	Empty Fields	Suspect Strength A1, A2, B	Common / Phonetic Candidate
Matching	Matching	Matching	Matching	Matching	TIN, Address, DOB, Last Name, First Name			A1	
Matching	Matching	Empty	Matching	Matching	TIN, Address, Last Name, First Name		DOB	A1	
Matching	Empty	Matching	Matching	Matching	TIN, DOB, Last Name, First Name		Address	A1	
Empty	Matching	Matching	Matching	Matching	Address, DOB, Last Name, First Name		TIN	A1	
Matching	Different	Matching	Matching	Matching	TIN, DOB, Last Name, First Name	Address		A1	
Matching	Empty	Empty	Matching	Matching	TIN, Last Name, First Name		Address, DOB	A1	
Matching	Different	Empty	Matching	Matching	TIN, Last Name, First Name	Address	DOB	A1	
Matching	Matching	Matching	Matching	Different	TIN, Address, DOB, Last Name	First Name		A2	Both
Matching	Matching	Different	Matching	Matching	TIN, Address, Last Name, First Name	DOB		A2	
Matching	Matching	Matching	Different	Matching	TIN, Address, DOB, First Name	Last Name		A2	Phonetic
Matching	Empty	Matching	Matching	Different	TIN, DOB, Last Name	First Name	Address	A2	Both
Matching	Matching	Empty	Matching	Different	TIN, Address, Last Name	First Name	DOB	A2	Both
Different	Matching	Matching	Matching	Matching	Address, DOB, Last Name, First Name	TIN		A2	
Matching	Different	Matching	Matching	Different	TIN, DOB, Last Name	Address, First Name		A2	Both
Empty	Matching	Matching	Different	Matching	Address, DOB, First Name	Last Name	TIN	A2	Phonetic
Matching	Matching	Empty	Different	Matching	TIN, Address, First Name	Last Name	DOB	A2	Phonetic
Matching	Empty	Matching	Different	Matching	TIN, DOB, First Name	Last Name	Address	A2	Phonetic
Matching	Different	Matching	Different	Matching	TIN, DOB, First Name	Address, Last Name		A2	Phonetic
Empty	Empty	Matching	Matching	Matching	DOB, Last Name, First Name		TIN, Address	A2	
Empty	Different	Matching	Matching	Matching	DOB, Last Name, First Name	Address	TIN	A2	
Empty	Matching	Empty	Matching	Matching	Address, Last Name, First Name		TIN, DOB	A2	
Matching	Matching	Matching	Different	Different	TIN, Address, DOB	Last Name, First Name		B	
Matching	Matching	Different	Matching	Different	TIN, Address, Last Name	DOB, First Name		B	

Figure 21: Example of Duplicate Suspect Processing Decision Matrix for Deterministic Matching

For the above matrix, additional matching rules are required to specify how the First Name / Middle Name logic must work and how the Last Name / Generational Suffix logic must work. For deterministic matching, it may also be beneficial to use compressed names (removing all non-alphanumeric characters) during the matching process. In addition, it may be valuable to invoke either common name (i.e., Bob vs Robert) and/or phonetic name logic for certain person suspects. These will all result in Data Matching rules.

Data Survivorship Rules define what data must be retained when two records in the MDM solution are deemed to be a match. A merge occurs when a record is being added and there is an existing record in the operational database that is identified as a match to the record being added. A collapse occurs when two records in the existing operational database are deemed to be a match. This may occur after a critical data element on one of the records is updated. Some criteria that are typically used to determine what data must be retained are:

- Most recent start date
- Oldest start date
- Most recent update date
- Lifecycle Status of the record (i.e., Current, Pending, Former, Rejected, Prospect, Discarded)
- Source System of the record (for merge)
- Type of the record (for merge) [for Customer domain, this may be Customer Role on Account)

Each applicable information requirement or information requirement group is analyzed to define the Data Survivorship rules, which includes defining what constitutes a duplicate for information requirement groups. Ensure that an Information Requirement exists for any criteria that is used in data survivorship.

Suspects: A data steward process may be put in place to proactively work the suspect records and either

- Collapse the suspects
- Correct erroneous or missing data in source systems, which would allow two records to collapse
- Mark two records as non-duplicates

Perform Business Process Analysis

Prior to performing the Business Process analysis, if the Extended Team is unfamiliar with the Front End Application systems, it may be valuable to conduct demonstrations.

Iteratively, analyze each Business Process identified during Alignment. The first step in the Business Process analysis is to create a generic To Be Process Map (agnostic of any specific Front End Application system). The To Be Process Map will have swim lanes for the Human Actor, Front End Application system, and the MDM Solution. Each swim lane will contain the activities performed by the respective actor. The To Be Process Map shows the interactions between the Human Actor and the Front End Application system, and the Front End Application system and the MDM Solution. Off page connectors can be used to show the relationship to other Business Processes.

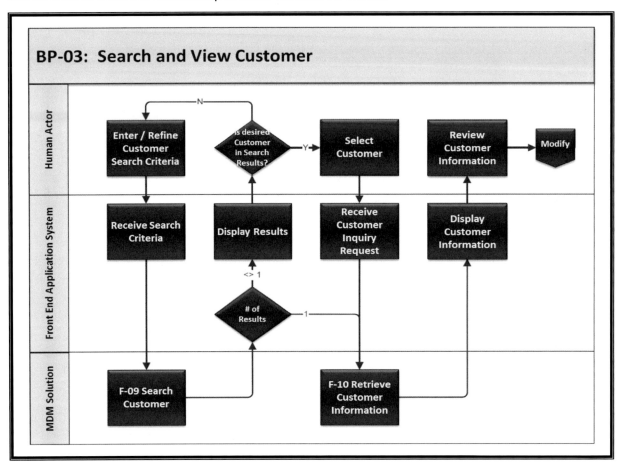

Figure 22: Example of To Be Process Map

The generic To Be Process Maps will serve as a guide for the Front End Application system development efforts. The Front End Application system development efforts will customize the generic To Be Process maps for their specific Front End Application system / process. A generic To Be Process Map may result in multiple To Be Process Maps for the Front End Application system. For example, Modify Customer may result in Modify Customer Profile Information, Modify Customer Preferences, and Modify Customer Contact Points.

Once the To Be Process Map is complete, the focus will shift to the activities in the MDM Solution swim lane and their interaction with the Front End Application system.

For each MDM activity:

- Define the inputs and outputs, at a high level (Information Requirement group level).
- Define any **Functional** business rules (i.e., Search Types, Search Criteria, Wildcards, etc.) the activities must enforce. Ensure these rules are included in the Business Rules catalog.
- Define **Data Update** business rules – where the Core MDM Function is setting or updating the value of an Information Requirement. Include these rules in the Business Rules catalog.

MDM activities with similar inputs, outputs, and business rules will be identified as a Core MDM Function. At the end of the Business Process analysis, analyze the MDM activities in the To Be Process Maps and identify the Core MDM Functions. It is valuable to consult with the architect during this process, as the Core MDM Functions are a key component of the MDM solution requirements and will define common or holistic software components for development. In a Services Oriented Architecture (SOA) the Core MDM Functions will define the candidate services. Once the Core MDM Functions are identified, the To Be Process Maps should be updated to reflect the Core MDM Function. For each Core MDM Function, the following information will be captured in the Requirements Catalog:

- Core MDM Function # - Unique Identifier for Core MDM Function
- Core MDM Function Name (verb noun format)
- Description for the Core MDM Function
- Business Processes the Core MDM Function supports
- Mode (whether the Core MDM Function will be Batch or Online (Services) or Both
- Criticality (see Information Requirements section for definitions)
- Complexity (set based off of related information requirements and business rules)

Inputs and outputs can either be captured in the Epics catalog or a **Functional** business rule created.

Epics - Core MDM Functions Catalog

Function	Core Function	High Level Description	Business Processes supported	Mode	Criticality	Complexity
F-01	Maintain Account	Process used to update Account information from source in mass. The process will	BP-01 Source Accounts	Batch	Critical	High
F-02	Establish Customer	Process used to add a Customer. Matching rules will be used to determine whether a	BP-10 Acquire Prospects	Batch and Online	Critical	High
F-03	Modify Customer Information	Process used to update Customer information. TIN and DOB cannot be updated using this	BP-04 Modify Customer	Batch and Online	Critical	Medium
F-04	Establish Account	Process used to add an Account. If a Customer Number is not present, the process will use	BP-06 Open Account	Batch and Online	Critical	High
F-05	Modify Account	Process used to update an Account. The following information may be included in request:	BP-07 Modify Account Information	Batch and Online	Critical	High
F-06	Transfer Account	Process used to transfer an Account from one Customer to another. This may be as a result	BP-08 Transfer Account	Batch and Online	Critical	Medium
F-07	Search Account	Process used to obtain a list of Accounts. The following criteria can be used to search:	BP-02 Search and View Account	Online	Important	High
F-08	Retrieve Account Information	Obtain information pertaining to an Account. This includes:	BP-02 Search and View Account	Online	Important	Medium
F-09	Search Customer	Process used to obtain a list of Customers. The following criteria can be used to search:	BP-03 Search and View Customer	Online	Medium	High
F-10	Retrieve Customer Information	Obtain information pertaining to a Customer. This includes:	BP-03 Search and View Customer	Online	Medium	Medium
F-11	Collapse Customers	Process used to collapse two Customers, that are actually the same Customer. The TIN or	BP-05 Collapse Customers	Online	Critical	High
F-12	Maintain Customer Grouping	Process used to modify Customer Grouping and Segmentation information. The	BP-04 Modify Customer	Batch and Online	Medium	Medium

Figure 23: Example of Epics Catalog - Core MDM Functions

A summary of the Business Processes should also be captured in the Requirements Catalog.

Business Processes Catalog

BP #	Business Process	High Level Description	Core MDM Functions required
BP-01	Source Accounts	The process used to load Customer information in a mass.	F-01 Maintain Account
BP-02	Search and View Account	The process used to find and obtain Account information.	F-07 Search Account
BP-03	Search and View Customer	The process used to find and obtain Customer information.	F-09 Search Customer
BP-04	Modify Customer Information	The process used to update Customer information for an existing Customer.	F-03 Modify Customer Information
BP-05	Open Account	The process used to establish an Account and Customer Role on Account.	F-04 Establish Account
BP-06	Modify Account Information	The process used to update Account information for an existing Account, includes	F-05 Modify Account
BP-07	Register User	The process used by customers to register for the internet. The MDM solution	F-07 Search Account
BP-08	Login User	The process used by customers to login to the internet or VRU. The MDM solution	F-10 Retrieve Customer Information
BP-09	Forgot Username	The process used by customer to retrieve a fogotten username. The MDM solution	F-07 Search Account
BP-13	Acquire Prospects	The process used to establish a Customer.	F-02 Establish Customer

Figure 24: Example of Business Processes Catalog

During this Business Process analysis, additional Information Requirements may be identified.

A Use Case diagram can be created to visually summarize the Business Processes and related Core MDM Functions. The Use Case diagram is a visual summary of the To Be Process Maps.

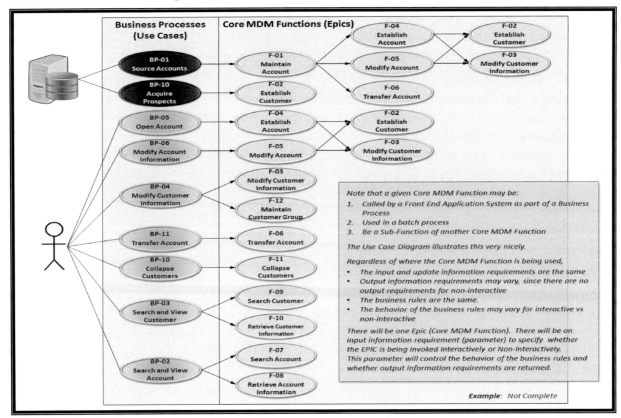

Figure 25: Example of Use Case Diagram (visual to summarize Business Processes and Core Functions)

Perform Entity Lifecycle Analysis (State Modeling)

For Entity Lifecycle Analysis, the statuses of the primary entity in the MDM domain are analyzed. There should be an information requirement for the Lifecycle Status, along with a corresponding Last Update date. If the Lifecycle Status values have not already been defined, define the possible values.

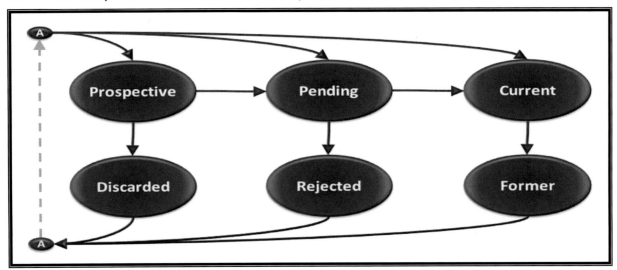

Figure 26: Example of Entity Lifecycle Status Diagram (State Diagram)

The Value Chain can be used as input for this activity. Business Processes should exist to take the status from one status to another. Additional **Business Processes** may be identified during this process. A **Data Update** business rule must be created to define how the Lifecycle Status is derived and updated. A decision matrix may be beneficial to complement the business rule.

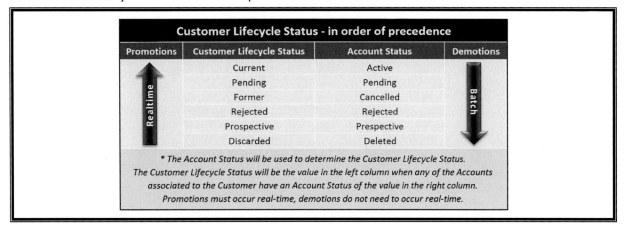

Figure 27: Example of Entity Lifecycle Status Decision Matrix for Data Update Rule

The Entity Lifecycle Status may be used for Data Survivorship rules, to limit search results, and as a dimension for operational and data quality metrics.

Define Operational and Data Quality Metrics

Next, identify and define the metrics that are required for the data stewards to monitor and proactively manage the MDM database from both an operational and a data quality perspective. There should not be a need to define metrics for invalid data, as it should be an objective **not** to add any invalid data to the MDM database. However, there may be data quality metrics identified to measure the completeness of the data or non-standard data. For example, a metric may be identified to monitor the number of customers who do not have a CASS standardized address or do not have a phone number. In addition to the metrics (what will be reported on), the dimensions must also be defined (how the metrics will be reported by). These metrics may ultimately be leveraged in an operational scorecard.

IR #	Name	Associated IR #	Data Element Type	Criticality
IR-101	**Customer Metrics**			
IR-101-01	Customer Type Code	IR-01-1	Dimension	Critical
IR-101-02	Customer Lifecycle Status Code	IR-01-8-1	Dimension	Critical
IR-101-03	Number of Customers		Metric	Critical
IR-101-04	Number of New Customers Added		Metric	Critical
IR-101-05	Number of Customers with more than 10 Names	IR-01-4	Metric	Critical
IR-101-06	Number of Persons with Names with unacceptable Special Characters	IR-01-4-1	Metric	Important
IR-101-07	Number of Persons without Birth Dates	IR-01-5-1	Metric	Important
IR-101-08	Number of Customers without Taxpayer Identification Number	IR-01-3-2	Metric	Critical
IR-101-09	Number of Customers with Non Standard Addresses	IR-02-1	Metric	Important
IR-101-10	Number of Customers with **only** Non Standard Addresses	IR-02-1	Metric	Critical
IR-101-11	Number of Customers with more than 10 Addresses	IR-02-1	Metric	Important
IR-101-12	Number of Customers without Phones	IR-02-2	Metric	Important
IR-101-13	Number of Customers with Non NANP Phones	IR-02-2	Metric	Important
IR-101-14	Number of Customers with **only** Non NANP Phones	IR-02-2	Metric	Important
IR-101-21	Number of Customers with more than 10 Phones	IR-02-1	Metric	Important
IR-101-22	Number of Customers without Email Addresses	IR-02-3	Metric	Important
IR-101-23	Number of Customers with more than 10 Email Addresses	IR-02-1	Metric	Important
IR-201	**Account Metrics**			
IR-301	**Customer Role Metrics**			

Table title: **Information Requirements Catalog - Metrics**

Figure 28: Example of Information Requirements Catalog for Operational and Data Quality Metrics

Describe Information Delivery Functions

Describe what information needs to be delivered to application systems. The Systems Context Diagram, created during Alignment, can be used to identify the Information Delivery functions. There are two types of Information Delivery functions:

- Extracts – Delivering the information in batch. This can include either a full extract or a delta file containing the changes since the last extract.

- Change Event Notifications – Delivering the information via Change Notifications, utilizing a "publish and subscribe" (pub/sub) architecture. The MDM solution would publish the fact that information has changed. Application systems can then subscribe to these change notifications and optionally apply the change to their system. A before and after image of the information should be included in the change notification, along with information that will allow receiving systems to filter out the records they are interested in. These changes could be a result of MDM updated information based on:

  - Information received from a Source System. An example may be where a new name, new address, or date of birth has been added. The consuming system can either automatically apply the update or may want to process these updates using workflow so that they can manually determine whether to apply the updates to their system or not. There may be additional processes that need to occur prior to applying any updates.
  - MDM process updates. This could be updating an address as a result of a periodic address standardization process or updating an enterprise number as a result of a collapse.

Define the following for each Information Delivery Functions:

- IDR # - Unique Identifier for Information Delivery Function
- Information Delivery Function Name
- Information Delivery Function Description
- The Information Requirements that should be included in the Information Delivery Functions. During Solution Scoping these will be defined at a high-level (Information Requirement Group).
- Type / Medium (i.e., Event Notification or Extract)
- Frequency
- Trigger – the MDM processes that can trigger the Change Event Notification
- Filters – that can be used by receiving application system to filter records

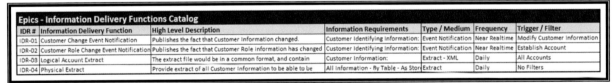

Epics - Information Delivery Functions Catalog						
IDR #	Information Delivery Function	High Level Description	Information Requirements	Type / Medium	Frequency	Trigger / Filter
IDR-01	Customer Change Event Notification	Publishes the fact that Customer Information changed.	Customer Identifying Information:	Event Notification	Near Realtime	Modify Customer Information
IDR-02	Customer Role Change Event Notification	Publishes the fact that Customer Role information has changed	Customer Identifying Information:	Event Notification	Near Realtime	Establish Account
IDR-03	Logical Account Extract	The extract file would be in a common format, and contain	Customer Information:	Extract - XML	Daily	All Accounts
IDR-04	Physical Extract	Provide extract of all Customer Information to be able to be	All Information - By Table - As Stor	Extract	Daily	No Filters

Figure 29: Example of Epics Catalog - Information Delivery Functions

Information Delivery functions are usually centered around a specific Subject Area, but may have Information Requirements from other Subject Areas. For example, in the Customer domain example, there may be Information Delivery functions at the Customer, Customer Role on Account, and Account level. The Customer Role on Account Information Delivery functions may have Customer Role on Account, Customer, and Account Information Requirements. When possible, common or holistic Information Delivery functions should be defined that can be leveraged by multiple application systems. When defining common Information Delivery functions, all applicable application systems must be analyzed to define the Information Requirements. In addition, additional Information Requirements may be included to support future requirements.

Describe Data Quality Functions

Identify and describe any Data Quality Functions that need to be performed periodically. There are two sources for these Data Quality Functions:

- Periodic Data Quality Functions, such as periodically processing all domestic addresses through address standardization or CASS certified software.

- Data Update rules that do not need to be performed in real-time. An example may be the Data Update rule for Lifecycle Status, if the demotion of the Lifecycle Status does not need to occur in real-time.

Define the following for each Data Quality Function:

- DQ # - Unique Identifier for Data Quality Function
- Data Quality Function Name
- Data Quality Function Description
- Trigger – the MDM processes that can trigger the Data Quality Function
- Filters – what records the Data Quality Process is ran for
- Frequency
- Criticality

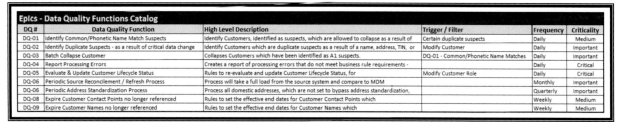

Epics - Data Quality Functions Catalog

DQ #	Data Quality Function	High Level Description	Trigger / Filter	Frequency	Criticality
DQ-01	Identify Common/Phonetic Name Match Suspects	Identify Customers, identified as suspects, which are allowed to collapse as a result of	Certain duplicate suspects	Daily	Medium
DQ-02	Identify Duplicate Suspects - as a result of critical data change	Identify Customers which are duplicate suspects as a result of a name, address, TIN, or	Modify Customer	Daily	Important
DQ-03	Batch Collapse Customer	Collapses Customers which have been identified as A1 suspects.	DQ-01 - Common/Phonetic Name Matches	Daily	Important
DQ-04	Report Processing Errors	Creates a report of processing errors that do not meet business rule requirements -		Daily	Critical
DQ-05	Evaluate & Update Customer Lifecycle Status	Rules to re-evaluate and update Customer Lifecycle Status, for	Modify Customer Role	Daily	Critical
DQ-06	Periodic Source Reconcilement / Refresh Process	Process will take a full load from the source system and compare to MDM		Monthly	Important
DQ-06	Periodic Address Standardization Process	Process all domestic addresses, which are not set to bypass address standardization,		Quarterly	Important
DQ-08	Expire Customer Contact Points no longer referenced	Rules to set the effective end dates for Customer Contact Points which		Weekly	Medium
DQ-09	Expire Customer Names no longer referenced	Rules to set the effective end dates for Customer Names which		Weekly	Medium

Figure 30: Example of Epics Catalog - Data Quality Functions

Define Non-Functional Requirements

Define any Non-Functional requirements. These will consist of:

- Audits and Controls
- Service Level Agreements – frequency and timing of updates, system availability, etc.
- Disaster and Data Recovery requirements
- Performance requirements
- Data Security and Visibility (governs the restriction of access to specific information)
- Authentication and Authorization requirements
  - Authentication is ensuring that the user / system is who they say they are
  - Authorization is ensuring that the user / system is permitted to access the system
- Capacity requirements

NFR #	Category (Performance / Security / Availability / Audit / Control)	Non-Functional Requirement
	Non-Functional Requirements Catalog	
NFR-01	Scheduled System Maintenance	Computer Operations requires scheduled maintenance for all systems to allow for backups, emergency fixes, and upgrades.
NFR-02	Authentication / Authorization - Online Systems	The Front End application systems are responsible for authenticating / authorizing the user of their Front End system.
NFR-03	Data Retention	Data Retention - Data must be maintained on-line for:
NFR-04	Audit and control	Interfaces (for critical inbound and outbound files) must utilize header and trailer records or control files to ensure
NFR-05	Performance	Performance SLA - to be met 95% of the time:
NFR-06	Batch Processing - Service Level Agreements	The turnaround time for DPIM processing a batch load file is as follows:

Figure 31: Example of Non-Functional Requirements

Capacity requirements should be captured for both the initial conversion and ongoing updates. For ongoing updates, capacity should be captured for both batch and online services. Online services capacity should be represented for peak hours and should also include the number of concurrent users.

Capacity Requirements	Deposits	Loans	Credit Cards	Life Insurance	Call Center	Branch Office	Internet	VRU	Total
Initial Conversion									
Accounts									
Customer Roles on Accounts									
Daily Updates									
New Accounts									
Changes to Existing Accounts									
Interactive Business Processes - Peak Hour									
Number of Concurrent Users									
BP-02 Search and View Account									
BP-03 Search and View Customer									
BP-04 Modify Customer Information									
BP-05 Open Account									
BP-06 Modify Account Information									
BP-07 Register User									
BP-11 Transfer Account									

Figure 32: Example of Capacity Requirements Matrix

Prioritize and Group Epics (Functions)

Once all Solution Scoping activities are complete, work with the extended team to prioritize and group the Epics (Functions) into logical groupings or bundles. This includes Core MDM Functions, Data Quality Functions, and Information Delivery Functions. This will serve as a starting point for the DDI (Design, Development, and Implementation) roadmap and also the order for defining the Functional Requirements. At a later time, a target release will be added, based on DDI estimates.

Priority	Epic #	Epic (Core MDM Function, Data Quality, Information Delivery)	Comments	Target Release
1	F-01	Maintain Account	Batch Orchestrator	R1
2	F-02	Establish Customer	Organization	R1
3	DQ-04	Report Processing Errors		R2
4	F-02	Establish Customer	Person	R2
5	F-04	Establish Account	Includes Customer Role on Account	R2
6	F-03	Modify Customer Information		R3
7	F-05	Modify Account	Includes Customer Role on Account	R3
8	F-06	Transfer Account		R3
9	DQ-03	Batch Customer Collapse		R4
10	F-09	Search Customer		R4
11	F-10	Retrieve Customer Information		R5
12	DQ-05	Evaluate & Update Customer Lifecycle Status		R5
13	DQ-06	Periodic Source Reconcilement / Refresh Process		R6
14	IDR-03	Logical Account Extract		R6
15	F-07	Search Account		R6
16	F-08	Retrieve Account Information		R7
17	DQ-02	Identify Duplicate Suspects as a result of critical data change	Result of TIN, DOB, Name, Addessr changes	R7
18	IDR-01	Customer Change Event Notification		R7
19	IDR-04	Physical Extract		R7
20	F-11	Collapse Customers		R6
21	F-12	Maintain Customer Grouping		R8
22	DQ-07	Periodic Address Standardization Process		R8
23	IDR-02	Customer Role Change Event Notification		R8
24	DQ-01	Identify Common/Phonetic Name Match Suspects		R9
25	DQ-08	Expire Customer Contact Points no longer referenced		R9
26	DQ-09	Expire Customer Names no longer referenced		R9

Figure 33: Example of Epic (Function) Priorities Matrix

Review and Approval of Solution Requirements

For the review, if the MDM solution is fairly extensive, it may be beneficial to develop an **Executive Summary** document for the sponsors and stakeholders not directly represented in the extended team. The Executive Summary would provide a summary of each work product produced, so that the sponsors and stakeholders get an overview of the solution without having to review each individual Information Requirement and Business Rule.   The Executive Summary would contain:

- Introduction, which would contain selected Business Requirements from Alignment, such as:
    - Problem / Opportunity Statement
    - Business Objectives
    - Critical Success Factors
- Overview
    - Overview of the MDM Solution
    - Summary of Solution Requirements Work Products produced during Solution Scoping
    - Features (prioritized and traced to Business Objectives and Stakeholder Needs)
- Actor Catalog
- Summary of Information Requirements – at an Information Requirement group level (the level of granularity is a judgement call), along with the details captured for each Information Requirement. It may also be beneficial to summarize the number of information requirements, by criticality. Additional Information Requirements work products and artifacts may be included:
    - Key Information Requirements, such as Type Codes that may be used as dimensions for the operational and data quality metrics, along with the corresponding Permitted Values.
    - Logical Data Model
    - A representative Logical Data Facsimile, with a link to all Logical Data Facsimiles
- Summary of Business Rules - by subject area, the number of business rules defined, along with the information captured for each Business Rule. It may also be valuable to call out key business rules:
    - Minimum Data Requirements
    - Key Matching Rules, along with what constitutes a match
- Entity Lifecycle Diagram – including statuses identified and how the status is derived
- Summary of Business Process analysis
    - Business Processes analyzed
    - Core MDM Functions Identified
    - Use Case Diagram – Visual Summary of Business Processes and Core MDM Functions
- Summary of Information Delivery Functions
- Summary of Data Quality Functions
- Key Non-Functional Requirements – work with Architect to identify which Non-Functional requirements to include in the Executive Summary
- Capacity requirements
- Out of Scope section – to highlight what is not included in the MDM Solution
- Related and Dependent Projects identified during Solution Scoping
- Consideration Analysis – summary of issues and decisions, including both key resolved issues (include action items that fostered a lot of discussion) and any outstanding issues, along with the owner. This will ensure the sponsors agree with the issue resolutions, decisions, and are comfortable with any remaining outstanding issues.
- Links to Work Products produced

This Executive Summary can either be in Word or PowerPoint format. The executive summary will serve as the basis for the review session. The approval process should go smoothly and be more of a formality, as the Extended Team participated in the development of the Solution Requirements and the Extended Team represents all Stakeholders.

Keys to Successful Solution Scoping

Some keys to successful Solution Scoping include:

- The Engagement Model, including architecture participation
- Ensuring the requirements are agnostic of any system
- Requirements visualizations, to complement and confirm written requirements
- Traceability – Epics (Functions), Information Requirements, and Business rules must trace back to Features, ensuring all Features have been accounted for and that there is no scope creep.
- Concurrent development of the Solution Architecture – including the MDM hub architecture (registry, repository, or hybrid) and the integration pattern(s) for each interface, component diagrams, etc. A variety of integration patterns can be used:
  - Batch (ETL) input (push or pull) – sourcing information
  - Near Real-time - Asynchronous (Fire and Forget)
  - Real-time - Synchronous (Interactive Services)
  - Batch Extracts – delivering information
  - Published Change Event Notifications (Pub/Sub) – notifying systems of updates
  These integration patterns may vary by system and can evolve over time.
- Maintaining an Action Item log for parking lot items identified during Solution Scoping sessions. Status should be reviewed at the beginning of each session. The Action Item log should include:
  - Date Identified
  - Description
  - Assigned to
  - Due Date
  - Status
  - Resolution
  - Completion Date
- A team space is a plus. The team space can be used to conduct:
  - The Extended Team facilitated sessions
  - Core Team preparation meetings and working sessions
  - Other Project Meetings (i.e., Project Status, Sponsor / Stakeholder meetings, etc.)
  In the team space, the following information can be posted on the walls:
  - Selected Alignment work products (Business Objectives, Stakeholder Needs, Features, etc.)
  - Solution Scoping calendar and agile task board (for status tracking)
  - Completed Solution Scoping visual work products (Logical Data Model, etc.)
  - White boards containing any work-in-progress
- A Requirements Management tool is a plus. A requirements management tool allows for:
  - Robust Traceability as the project proceeds into functional requirements, allowing
    - Information Requirements to be traced to Epics (Functions) [and User Stories]
    - Business Rules to be traced to Epics (Functions) [and User Stories]
    - Information Requirements to be traced to Business Rules
  - Integration of additional details during functional requirements, such as logic flows and decision matrices
  - While a Requirements Management tool is a plus, depending on the tool, it may be better to develop the Requirements Catalog in Excel and load the information into the Requirements Management tool at the end of Solution Scoping. This is because the ability to make global or mass changes may be limited in the tool and more efficient in Excel. In addition, presentation may be easier and summary information may be cleaner in Excel.

Elaboration – Functional Requirements – Epics

After Solution Scoping, the next step is to detail out the requirements for each Epic (Function), including Core MDM Functions, Data Quality Functions, and Information Delivery Functions. During this process, associated actors, inputs, outputs, data updates, and associated business rules are defined and an activity diagram is produced. Functional requirements should be done iteratively, based on the priority assigned during Solution Scoping. For each Epic, the following activities should be completed.

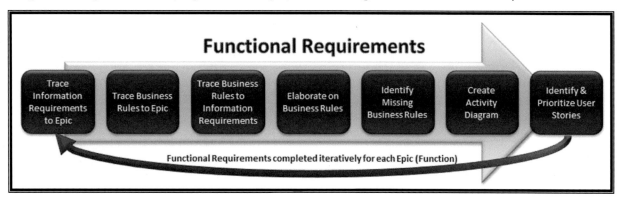

Figure 34: Elaboration [Functional Requirements – Epic] Activities

Trace Information Requirements to Epic (Function)

Based on the high level inputs and outputs identified while developing the To Be Process Maps, and the applicable business rules, trace the individual Information Requirements to the Epic (Function). Identify which Information Requirements are input to, output from, and updated by the Epic (Function). Updated by should only include those Information Requirements that the MDM solution sets or alters. Data Update business rules should exist for all Information Requirements that are updated by the Epic. The input and output requirements for the Epic (Function) will be used to design the interface layouts.

Information Requirements Catalog

IR #	Name	Description	Rationale (Purpose)	Data Element Type	Criticality	Deposits	Loans	Credit Card	Life Insurance	Secure?	F-02 Input	F-02 Output	F-02 Update	F-03 Input	F-03 Output	F-03 Update	F-09 Input	F-09 Output	F-10 Org Output	F-10 Person Output
IR-01	Customer Profile Information	Data used to describe Customer and enable identification.	360 View, Auditing.			✓	✓	✓	✓											
IR-01-1	Customer Type Code	Identifies if the Customer is a Person or Organization.	Identifying, Matching	Code	Critical	✓	✓	✓	✓	✓	R1	R2		R3	R3		R4	R4	R5	R5
IR-01-2	Customer Number	A unique number assigned to each Customer.			Critical							R2	R2	R3	R3		R4	R4	R5	
IR-01-3	Customer Tax Identification	Data relating to the Tax Identification for the Customer.				✓	✓	✓	✓											
IR-01-3-1	Customer Taxpayer Identification Type	Represents the type of Taxpayer Identification Number.	Identifying	Code	Critical	✓	✓				R1			R3			R4	R4	R5	R5
IR-01-3-2	Customer Taxpayer Identification Numb	Number used to identify a Customer for U.S. Tax Reporting	Identifying, Matching	Number	Critical	✓	✓			Mask	R1			R3			R4	R4	R5	R5
IR-01-3	Customer Name	Data relating to the Name(s) of the Customer.				✓	✓	✓	✓											
IR-01-4-1	Person Name	Data specific to the name for a Person.				✓	✓	✓	✓											
IR-01-4-1-01	Person Name Type Code	Represents the type of name used by a Person.	Communication	Code	Critical	✓	✓		✓		R2			R3						R5
IR-01-4-1-02	Prefix Type Code	Component of a Person Name representing a title that	Communication	Code	Important	✓	✓		✓		R2			R3				R4		R5
IR-01-4-1-03	First Name	Component of a Person Name representing the first given	Identifying	Name	Critical	✓	✓	✓	✓		R2			R3			R4	R4		R5
IR-01-4-1-04	Middle Name	Component of a Person Name representing the second given	Identifying	Name	Critical	✓	✓	✓	✓		R2			R3			R4	R4		R5
IR-01-4-1-05	Last Name	Component of a Person Name representing the surname or	Identifying	Name	Critical	✓	✓	✓	✓		R2			R3			R4	R4		R5
IR-01-4-1-06	Generational Suffix Type Code	Component of a Person Name representing a way to	Identifying	Code	Critical	✓	✓	✓	✓		R2			R3			R4	R4		R5
IR-01-4-1-07	Professional Suffix Type Code	Component of a Person Name representing a Professional	Communication	Code	Nice	✓	✓		✓		R2			R3				R4		R5
IR-01-4-1-08	Preferred Name Indicator	Indicates the name by which a person prefers to be	Communication	Indicator	Critical	✓					R2			R3				R4		
IR-01-4-2	Organization Name	Data specific to the name for an Organization or Team.				✓	✓	✓												
IR-01-5	Customer Person Information	Individuals will be stored as Persons				✓	✓	✓	✓	✓										
IR-01-6	Customer Organization Information	Sole Proprietor, Partnership/LLC, and Corporations will be				✓	✓	✓												
IR-01-8	Customer Lifecycle	Data that has been identified but needs to be discussed in																		
IR-02	Customer Contact Point Information	Data used to enable interaction with Customer.	Auditing.			✓	✓	✓	✓											
IR-02-1	Customer Postal Address	Data that is specific to the Postal Address of the Customer.				✓	✓	✓	✓											
IR-02-2	Customer Phone	Data that is specific to the Phone of the Customer.				✓	✓	✓	✓											
IR-02-3	Customer Email Address	Data that is specific to the Email Address of the Customer.				✓	✓	✓	✓											
IR-02-4	Customer Website	Data that is specific to the Website of the Customer.				✓	✓													
IR-02-5	Customer Social Media	Data that is specific to the Social Media of the Customer.				✓	✓													
IR-03	Account Summary	Data relating to the Agreement with the Customer.	360 View, Routing.			✓	✓	✓												
IR-04	Account to Account Relationship	Data relating to the Relationships between two Accounts.	360 View, Auditing.			✓	✓	✓												
IR-05	Customer Role on Account	Data relating to the Role the Customer is playing on the	360 View, Auditing.			✓	✓	✓	✓											
IR-06	Customer to Customer Relationship	Data relating to the Relationships between two Customers.	360 View, Auditing.			✓	✓	✓												
IR-07	Customer Grouping	Data relating to a Groupings of Customers.	360 View, Auditing.			✓	✓	✓	✓											
IR-08	Customer Segmentation	Data relating to a Segmentation of Customers.	360 View, Auditing.						✓											
IR-09	Customer Preference	Data Related to a Customer Preference	Auditing.			✓	✓													

Figure 35: Example of Information Requirements to Epic (Function) Traceability Matrix (IOU Matrix)

The Input / Output / Update traceability matrix (IOU matrix) can be included in the Information Requirements catalog. As the project progresses, the traceability matrix can be used to capture the release the information requirement is implemented for each Epic (Function). The example shows release information entered. Prior to the release there would just be an "X" in the columns.

Trace Business Rules and NFRs to Epic (Function)

Next identify which business rules and non-functional requirements (NFRs) apply to the Epic (Function).

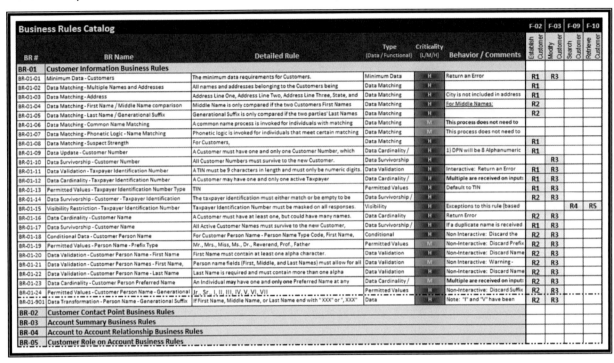

Figure 36: Example of Business Rules / NFRs to Epic (Function) Traceability Matrix

The Business Rules / NFRs to Epic (Function) traceability matrix can be included in the Business Rules catalog. Similar to the Information Requirements to Epic (Function) traceability matrix (IOU matrix), as the project progresses, the traceability matrix can be used to capture the release the business rule is implemented for each Epic. A business rule may be implemented in multiple releases for a given Epic, if something changes in the business rule. The example shows release information entered. Prior to the release there would just be an "X" in the columns.

Trace Business Rules to Information Requirements

Next, optionally trace each of the Business Rules associated with the Epic (Function) to the appropriate Information Requirements. If the Business Rule was associated to an earlier Epic (Function), this step is not required, as it should already have been completed. This step is **not** essential for functional requirements; however, it does provide value. Tracing the Business Rules to the Information Requirements will help identify missing business rules, support User Story card development, and support impact analysis going forward. This step is fairly straight forward when using a Requirements Management tool; however, can also be completed in the Requirements Catalog, when not using a Requirements Management tool.

There are three options to accomplish this in the Requirements Catalog:

Requirements for an MDM Solution

1. The first option is to integrate Business Rule tracing in the Information Requirements catalog, with a column for each Business Rule type. With this option, enter the Business Rule number for each applicable Business Rule in the appropriate cell. Multiple Business Rules may exist for a given Information Requirement / Business Rule type. With this option, the primary information for the Information Requirement, the Information Requirements to Epic (Function) matrix (IOU matrix) and Information Requirements to Business Rule matrix can all be collapsible, making the catalog easier to work with.

Figure 37: Example of Information Requirements to Business Rules Traceability Matrix

2. The second option is to integrate Business Rule tracing in the Information Requirements catalog using one column for all associated Business Rules. The number of Business Rules associated to a given Information Requirement can make this option challenging.

3. The third option is to integrate Information Requirements tracing into the Business Rules catalog using one column for all associated Information Requirements. The number of Information Requirements associated to a given Business Rule can make this option challenging.

Elaborate on Business Rules

Verify the business rules that are traced to the Epic (Function) are correct and complete. Add decision matrices or decision flow diagrams to complement complex business rules and elaborate on behavior if necessary. In addition, create any post conditions / error messages for the business rule. It is a good practice to have a guideline for how to format error messages for consistency, for example:

Rule Type	Error Message Guideline
Minimum Data and Conditional Minimum Data	Missing Data – [Information Requirement Name]
Data Validation	Invalid Data - [Business Rule Summary]
Permitted Values	Invalid Data – [Information Requirement Name]
Data Integrity	Data Integrity Error – [Business Rule Summary]
Data Cardinality	Data Cardinality Error – [Business Rule Summary]
Functional	[Business Rule Summary]

Error messages for Information Requirements that repeat require additional context information for the error. The context information will be the information requirements that uniquely identify the repeating information requirement or information requirement group. Some rule types may not have error messages – for example some Data Integrity and Permitted Value rules may choose to default a value, as opposed to error, when an invalid value is received; and Data Cardinality rules of "may have zero to many" will not produce an error. In addition, there are some functional rule types that will not produce error messages, such as Data Matching, Data Survivorship, Data Transformation, and Data Update rules.

Business Rules Catalog					
BR #	BR Name	Detailed Rule	Type (Data / Functional)	Behavior / Comments	Post Conditions / Error Messages
BR-01	Customer Information Business Rules				
BR-01-11	Data Validation - Taxpayer Identification Number	A TIN must be 9 characters in length and must	Data Validation	Return Error	E1 - Invalid Data - Taxpayer Identification Number
BR-01-12	Data Cardinality - Taxpayer Identification Number	A Customer may have one and only one active	Data Cardinality /	Multiple are	E1 - Data Cardinality Error - only one Taxpayer Identification Number allow
BR-01-13	Permitted Values - Taxpayer Identification	TIN	Permitted Values	Default to TIN	A1 - Value TIN is received
BR-01-14	Data Survivorship - Customer - Taxpayer Identification	The taxpayer identification must either match or be empty to be identified as a match. If either Customer (or both) has a Taxpayer	Data Survivorship / Data Update		A1 - Both Customers have Taxpayer Identification Number A2 - One Customer has Taxpayer Identification Number, one does not A3 - Neither Customer has Taxpayer Identification Number
BR-01-15	Visibility Restriction - Taxpayer Identification	Taxpayer Identification Number must be	Visibility	Exceptions to this	A1 - Consumer does not have access, TIN is masked
BR-01-16	Data Cardinality - Customer Name	A Customer must have at least one, but could	Data Cardinality	Return Error	E1 - Data Cardinality Error - at least one Customer Name is required
BR-01-17	Data Survivorship - Customer Name	All Active Customer Names must survive to the	Data Survivorship /	If a duplicate name	A1 - No Duplicate Customer Names
BR-01-18	Conditional Data - Customer Person Name	For Customer Person Name - Person Name Type Code, First Name, and Last Name are required.	Conditional Minimum Data	Return Error	E1 - Missing Data - First Name E2 - Missing Data - Last Name

Figure 38: Example of adding Post Conditions / Error Messages to Business Rules Catalog

Identify any missing Business Rules

Take time to ensure all business rules have been identified. Solution Scoping was performed to a depth to ensure stakeholders were aligned and to allow for multiple concurrent development efforts. This means that every business rule may not have been identified and defined during Solution Scoping. During Functional Requirements, with the focus on a specific Epic (Function), ensure there are no missing Business Rules. Review the identified business rules, the related information requirements, along with the business rule types to ensure there are no missing business rules. The Information Requirements to Business Rules traceability matrix can assist in this process.

Complete Activity Diagram for Epic (Function)

Complete an Activity Diagram for each Epic (Function), which highlights the logical flow. The activity diagram should be a high level flow and depict what logically has to occur within the Epic (Function). It is **not** intended to represent the design of the Epic (Function). It will define the logical paths for the Epic (Function). Activity Diagrams should be completed for both Core MDM Functions and Data Quality Functions; however, may not be necessary for Information Delivery Functions due to their simplicity.

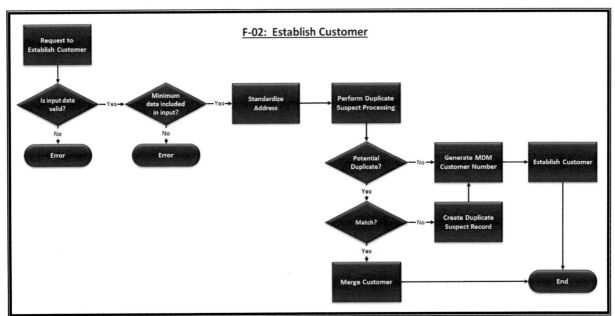

Figure 39: Example of Activity Diagram for Epic (Core MDM Function)

Identify User Stories for Epic (Function)

Finally, the Epic (Function) is broken down into User Stories, based on:

- The logical paths defined in the Activity Diagram for the Epic (Function)
- Optional Subject Areas or Information Requirement Groups within the Epic (Function)

The User Stories for an MDM solution are more technical than a typical User Story; this is because the user is a system as opposed to a person. The level of granularity for the User Story breakdown will depend on the complexity of the Epic (Function). The User Story should be broken down small enough to allow for it to be completely delivered in an iteration. For example, the F-02 Establish Customer Epic (Function) might be broken down into the following User Stories:

- F-02 Establish Customer with minimum data, which results in an add
- F-02 Establish Customer with minimum data, which results in a merge
- F-02 Establish Customer with minimum data, which results in a suspect
- F-02 Establish Customer with optional Phone information, which results in an add
- F-02 Establish Customer with optional Phone information, which results in a merge
- F-02 Establish Customer with optional other Contact Point information, which results in an add
- F-02 Establish Customer with optional other Contact Point information, which results in a merge
- F-02 Establish Customer with optional Customer information, which results in an add
- F-02 Establish Customer with optional Customer information, which results in a merge
- F-02 Establish Customer with all possible information, which results in an add
- F-02 Establish Customer with all possible information, which results in a merge

In the above example, Phone may be broken out as a separate User Story, because of the number of associated business rules. Whereas Email Address, Social Media, and Website may be combined into one user story, because they are simpler and are similar. If preferred, the user story can be formatted as follows: "As a Source System, I want to Establish a Customer with minimum data, which results in an add when no customer match is found". The identified User Stories should be prioritized based on dependencies and business value, and do not necessarily need to be delivered in the same release. For agile development, these user stories are incorporated into the product backlog.

Review and Approval of Functional Requirements

Once the Functional Requirements are complete for the Epic (Function), they must be reviewed and approved by the identified participants. This should include:

- Business Lead
- Data Specialist
- Technical Lead
- QA / Test Lead
- Architect (optional)
- Extended Team (optional)
- Applicable Developers (if identified)
- Applicable QA / Test Analyst (if identified)

Depending on the organization, the Architect may be a participant. Depending on the Epic (Function), members from the Extended Team may also need to participate. The timing of the review is key. For agile development, the review should occur 2-3 iterations prior to development, allowing time for approval, to elaborate on the User Stories, and to complete any design activities, without being too far in advance that the team is not ready to focus on the Epic review. For traditional development, the review can be completed 1-2 weeks prior to design, allowing time for approval.

Functional Requirements – Key Concurrent Activities

At the same time as functional requirements are kicking off, there are some non-requirements foundational activities that should occur:

Preliminary Data Mapping and Data Profiling

Preliminary data mapping and data profiling can begin for key Source systems (Core Processing systems) as soon as the Information Requirements are defined in Solution Scoping. For each Source system, preliminary data mapping will be completed, mapping the Source data elements to the Information Requirements and defining preliminary Data Transformation rules. Once the preliminary data mapping is completed, preliminary data profiling can be completed. The preliminary data profiling should analyze source data elements for the following:

- Conformance to Business Rules
- Minimum and Maximum data values
- Analysis for Null values
- Analysis of Frequent values (i.e., top 5 or top 10 values)
- Length of information – shortest and longest
- Pattern (or format) analysis

The preliminary data profiling may result in additional **Data Transformation Rules** or additions to **Permitted Values** for a Permitted Value Rule. Comprehensive Data Mapping and Data Profiling will occur as part of the Sourcing efforts. A data mapping and a data profiling work product should be produced and maintained for each source system.

Physical Data Model / Mapping

The physical data model / mapping should occur directly after Solution Scoping concludes, to provide the technical roadmap for the information requirements. The Physical Data Model / Mapping may result in **System Rules**. This may occur when the information requirement is mapped to a generic table, there may be a need to set a type code value to identify the specific information requirement.

Common Interface Layout Design

A Common Interface Layout should be designed shortly after Solution Scoping concludes; it should be lagged slightly to allow the initial Functional Requirements iteration to be underway. This interface layout will be used to source information from and provide information to application systems.

Application Framework

Finally, based on the Core MDM Functions and Integration Patterns / Component Design outlined in the Solution Architecture, an overall application framework should be establish directly after Solution Scoping and prior to application design and development. This is key for a smooth development effort and to minimize rework.

Sourcing efforts and Front-End development efforts

Sourcing efforts may begin at the same time as functional requirements for the MDM solution. Front-End development efforts should wait to begin until after Functional Requirements are completed for the key Epics (Core MDM Functions) required for the Front End application system.

Elaboration of User Stories

For agile development, each User Story will be elaborated on and a User Story card created:

Trace Information Requirements and Business Rules to User Story

The appropriate input, output, and update Information Requirements will be traced to the User Story. The Information Requirements for the Epic will be the starting point for this activity. The Information Requirements for the User Story will be a subset of the Information Requirements for the Epic.

The appropriate Business Rules and Non-Functional Requirements should be traced to the User Story. The Business Rules and NFRs for the Epic will be the starting point for this activity. The Business Rules and NFRs for the User Story will be a subset of the Business Rules and NFRs for the Epic.

Identify Scenarios for each User Story

For each User Story, there may be multiple scenarios. These scenarios may be broken down based on:

- Optional input
- For Information Requirements that repeat, one occurrence versus multiple occurrences
- The behaviors and post conditions (errors or warnings) defined for the associated Business Rules

Define Acceptance Criteria for each Scenario in the User Story

The acceptance criteria for each scenario must be defined. This can be written in the form of Gherkin: Given <Context or Pre-conditions>, When <Action>, Then <Observable Outcomes, including Assertions>. For example, for the User Story "F-02 Establish Customer with minimum data, which results in an add" the acceptance criteria may be "Given a customer match does not exist in the database, When a request is received to Establish a new customer, Then a new customer will be added to the database".

Keys to Success for MDM Agile Development

There are several keys to successful agile development for MDM solutions:

- Do not overlook design. Prior to starting development for the stories within a specific Epic (Function), play a design card to ensure there is structure for all subsequent development cards. It is important not to overlook the importance of application design for an MDM solution. Design cards may result in additional Data Quality functions, System Rules required to support the MDM system, and System Information Requirements required to support processing.
- The requirements analyst, developers, and test analysts should have a specialty. This may be based on Epic (Function) or Subject Area within Epic. Without this, a substantial amount of time will be spent getting oriented to the User Story. In addition, without understanding of the prior stories played for the given Epic or Subject Area, it is possible that the development for the story is not integrated properly, thereby causing prior logic to error. While a "journeyman" concept may work great for a User Interface development effort (where the next available resource picks up the next available User Story), it causes overhead and rework for MDM development efforts.
- Take care not to break the Epics (Functions) down into too small of User Stories. Each User Story should tell a complete story. Breaking the User Stories down too small causes overhead.

Note that for traditional iterative / incremental development, the development is based directly off of the functional requirements for the Epic and there is no need to elaborate on the User Stories.

Test Scenarios

The test analyst will subsequently define **Functional** Test Scenarios. For agile development, the Test Scenarios will be based on the Acceptance Criteria. For traditional development, the Test Scenarios will be based on User Stories and Business Rules. There can be multiple Test Scenarios for a given User Story. The Functional Test Scenarios will trace back to the Epic (Function), User Story, and Business Rule.

In addition to the Functional Test Scenarios, **Data Characteristic** Test Scenarios should be written that analyze the populated MDM database to ensure the Minimum Data, Conditional Minimum Data, Data Validation, Data Integrity, Permitted Values, and Data Transformation business rules are consistently being enforced. The Data Characteristic Test Scenarios will trace back to the Business Rule.

Change Management

Once a Work Product is approved and baselined, it is critical to process any changes to the Work Product through a Change Management Process and **communicate** approved change requests to the entire team. Communication is essential for all aspects of an MDM development effort due to the number of participants, especially regarding changes. Approvers may vary, depending on the Work Product.

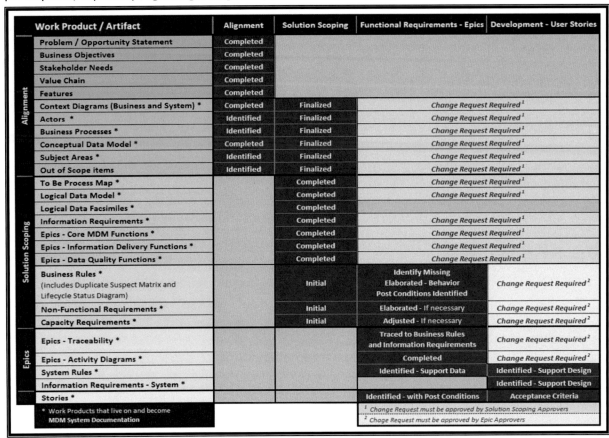

Figure 40: Work Product - Change Management Matrix

Solution Scoping change requests must be estimated, prioritized, and added to the Epics Priority Matrix after approval. **Functional Requirements changes** that impact the intent of the requirement or the development effort must be added to a Change Log after approval. In addition, User Story Cards must be created for agile development. These User Story cards must be added to the backlog and prioritized accordingly. **Clarifications** which do not impact the intent of the requirement or the development effort should be communicated; however, require no further action. The Change Log should contain:

- Work Product Artifact changed
  - Work Product Traceability Number / Unique Identifier (i.e., Business Rule Number)
  - Work Product Artifact description (i.e., Business Rule Description)
- Change Request Number
- Change Request Approval Date
- Change Description

- Target Release
- Associated User Story Card (for agile development)
- Status

Traceability

Vertical Traceability

Vertical Traceability traces requirements work product artifacts across the Solution Development Lifecycle, which ensures all requirements are accounted for in the solution (i.e., completeness of the solution) and that all development traces back to a requirement (i.e., no scope creep). The following diagram summarizes the vertical traceability.

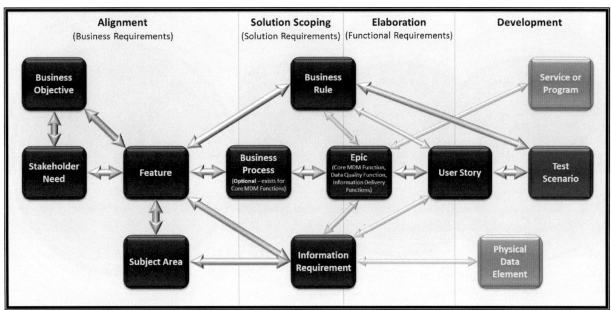

Figure 41: Vertical Traceability

During Alignment (Business Requirements), the following are traced:

Stakeholder Needs to Business Objectives: Each Stakeholder Need should trace to a Business Objective. If it does not, either there is a missing business objective or the stakeholder need is not valid.

Features to Business Objectives and Stakeholder Needs: Each feature must trace to at least one business objective and at least one stakeholder need. If it does not, either there is a missing business objective / stakeholder need or the feature is not valid. In addition, each business objective / stakeholder need must trace to at least one feature. If not, there is a feature missing.

During Solution Scoping (Solution Requirements), the following are traced:

Epics (Functions), Information Requirements, and Business Rules to Features: Epics (Functions), Information Requirements, and Business rules must all trace back to Features, ensuring that there is no scope creep. In addition, some Non-Functional requirements will also trace back to Features. Each Feature must have at least one Solution Requirement Work Product artifact tracing back to it, ensuring all Features have been accounted for.

During Elaboration (Functional Requirements), User Stories are traced to Epics (Functions).

During Development, Test Scenarios are traced back to the Epic, User Story, and Business Rule, ensuring all functionality is tested. In addition, Epics can optionally be traced to Services or Programs and Information Requirements can optionally be traced to the Physical Data Elements.

Horizontal Traceability

Horizontal Traceability shows how the various requirements work product artifacts relate to each other, which facilitates ongoing impact analysis. The following diagram summarizes the horizontal traceability.

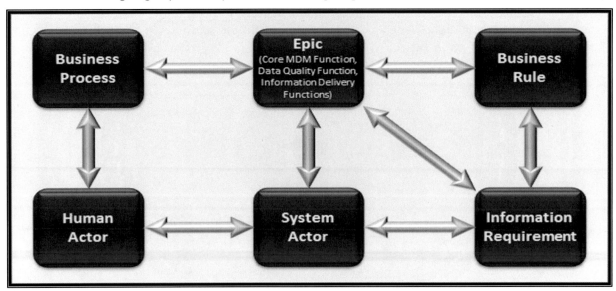

Figure 42: Horizontal Traceability

Horizontal Traceability is established during Solution Scoping (Solution Requirements) and Elaboration (Functional Requirements), and will answer the following questions, to support impact analysis:

- What Business Processes are performed by a Human Actor
- What System Actors a Human Actor uses
- What Epics (Functions) are executed by a System Actor
- What Epics (Functions) comprise a Business Process
- What Business Rules and Non-Functional Requirements an Epic (Function) enforces
- What Information Requirements are Input, Output or Updated by an Epic (Function)
- What Information Requirements are required to enforce a specific Business Rule
- What Information Requirements are determined by a specific Business Rule
- What Information Requirements are sourced by a specific System Actor
- What Information Requirements are consumed by a specific System Actor

In addition, tracing the Business Rules to the Information Requirements can also help to identify missing business rules.

The purpose of traceability, including both Vertical and Horizontal Traceability is to:

1. ensure all Business Objectives have been met
2. ensure all requirements are accounted for in the solution (i.e., completeness of the solution)
3. ensure all development activities trace back to a requirement (i.e., no scope creep)
4. elaborate on Functional Requirements, by associating Information Requirements, Business Rules, and Actors to Epics (Functions)
5. assist in identifying missing work product artifacts
6. support ongoing impact analysis

When a Requirements Management tool is leveraged, traceability also provides a method to navigate the various requirements work product artifacts.

Summary

Summary of Requirements Approach for an MDM Solution

To summarize the requirements approach for an MDM solution:

- The first step is to gain <u>Alignment</u> on what is to be achieved by the MDM effort.
- The next step is to conduct an upfront <u>Solution Scoping</u> effort, establishing the foundation (blueprint) for the MDM solution. Concurrently, the Solution Architecture should be completed.
- Next, <u>Functional Requirements</u> are iteratively elaborated on for each <u>Epic</u> (Function). Concurrently, sourcing efforts and front-end development efforts may begin.
- Finally, <u>User Stories</u> are identified and elaborated upon for each Epic (Function), along with the acceptance criteria. The acceptance criteria is traced to Test Scenarios.

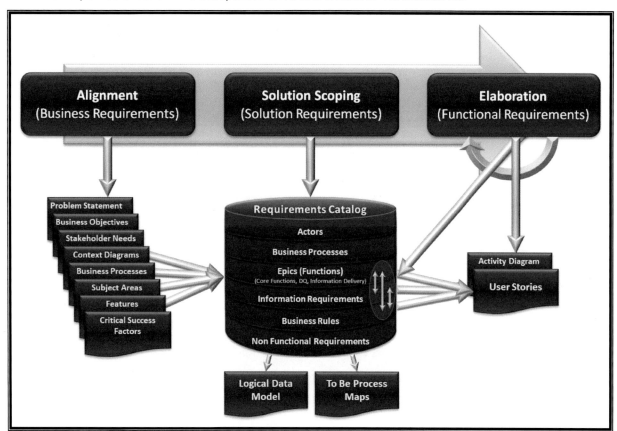

Figure 43: Overview of MDM Requirements Process

The Solution Requirements must have enough depth to ensure:

- Stakeholders are aligned on the solution, prior to investment
- Requirements are comprehensive, based on key source systems, to minimize rework
- There is a clear and common understanding of the solution requirements, prior to kicking off multiple concurrent development efforts

The output is a repository of reusable requirements work products, where the individual work product artifacts can be related to each other to form the Functional Requirements. This repository of requirements work product artifacts not only facilitates and promotes reuse, it also ensures consistency. This repository will become the systems documentation for the MDM solution, after implementation.

Without an upfront solution scoping effort to establish a strong foundation (blueprint), there can be churn in the requirements process and costly rework in the development process. This occurs when new or changed requirements are discovered as new systems are integrated into the MDM solution.

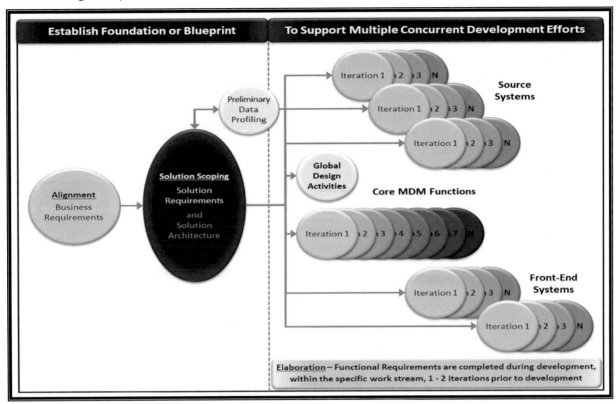

Figure 44: Requirements Approach - Importance of Upfront Solution Scoping

The requirements work products produced can be categorized by the focus of the requirements work product (goals, data, process, actors). Below is a matrix which shows the requirements work products by requirements level (or solution development lifecycle phase) and requirements focus:

👁 - Visual Requirements Work Products *(a picture is worth a thousand words)*		Requirements Focus			
		Goals	**Data**	**Process**	**Actors**
SDLC Phases / Requirements Levels	**Alignment** Business Requirements	Problem / Opportunity Statement	Subject Areas	Business Process List	Business and System Context Diagrams 👁
		Business Objectives	Conceptual Data Model 👁		Preliminary Actor Catalog
			Stakeholder Needs		
			Features *(Prioritized)*		
	Solution Scoping Solution Requirements		Information Requirements	Business Process Details	Finalized Actor Catalog
			Data Quality Rules	Functional Rules	
			Duplicate Suspect Processing Rules		
			Logical Data Model 👁	To Be Process Maps 👁	
			Logical Data Facsimile 👁	Functions List *(Prioritized)*	
	Elaboration Functional Requirements		Functional Requirements (by Epic / Function) *		
			Associated Information Requirements to Functions (Inputs, Outputs, Updates)	Activity Diagram 👁	Associated Actors
			Associated Business Rules to Functions and Information Requirements		
			User Stories List *(Prioritized)*		

Figure 45: Requirements Work Products Matrix, by Requirements Level and Requirements Focus

How does an MDM Requirements approach differ

Requirements gathering and documentation activities are similar, regardless of the type of solution. What differs is the approach, the emphasis of specific activities, and the content of work products. For example, for both Master Data Management efforts and Data Warehouse / Reporting efforts, there is more emphasis on Information Requirements; whereas for Front End Application system development, there is more emphasis on Business Processes and To Be Process Maps, and for Core Processing systems there is more emphasis on Business Processes and Business Rules. Below is a table that outlines some of the differences in requirements gathering and documentation approach, based on solution type.

Type of Solution	Activity Focus
Master Data Management	• Identify Subject Areas during Alignment • For new systems, initial Solution Scoping phase required to establish foundation / blueprint • Focus is on **Comprehensive Information Requirements and Data Quality** • To Be Process Maps exist for business processes that either maintain or access the information • To Be Process Maps will detail out both interactions between Human Actor and Front End Systems, and Front End Systems with Master Data Management Solution • Business Rules include both Functional and Data Quality rules
Data Warehouse / BI Reporting	• Identify Subject Areas during Alignment • For new systems, initial Solution Scoping phase required to establish foundation / blueprint • Focus is on **Information Delivery Requirements and Data Usability** • It is critical to understand what questions must be answered by the data • To Be Process Maps are simple and are comprised of data load and information delivery • Information Requirements must be categorized – Metrics, Dimensions, or Attributes • Business Rules are primarily Data Quality rules
Core Processing System	• Solution Scoping can be more iterative • Emphasis is on **Business Processes and Business Rules** • Business Processes will include many temporal (time driven) processes • Information Requirements are defined as part of To Be Process modeling and Functional Requirements • Temporal processes <u>may not</u> require To Be Process Maps, but will have Information Requirements and Business Rules
Front End Application	• Solution Scoping can be iterative and less structured • Focus is on **Business Processes and To Be Process maps** • Process Maps exist for business processes that either maintain or access the information • Process Maps will focus on interactions between Human Actor and Front End System • Information Requirements are defined as part of To Be Process modeling and Functional Requirements • Detailed Requirements will include UX Design

Figure 46: Summary of Requirements Approach differences by Type of Solution

Key Qualities for an MDM Requirements Analyst

Finally, below are some traits that make a good requirements analyst for an MDM project:

- Good Listening Skills: Working with individuals from a variety of business areas, with different terminology, will require the analyst to be able to determine when individuals are referring to the same or different information; being able to distinguish the two is essential.

- Inquisitiveness: Asking the right questions to elicit the requirements information is imperative to ensure everyone has a common understanding.

- Detailed and Data Oriented: Consistency in terminology and traceability are two keys for MDM solutions. Attention to detail is a must.

- Technically Oriented: MDM solutions are more technical than other types of systems. This is because it is System Actors, as opposed to Human Actors, that are interacting with the solution.

About the Author

Vicki is a requirements analyst, with more than 33 years of experience in information technology. She began her career as a programmer / analyst and over the years has held various positions within information technology including:

- *Project / Program Manager*
- *Application Development Manager*
- *Test Coordinator*
- *Requirements Analyst*

The last 15 years has been primarily focused on requirements.

Vicki has more than 25 years of experience working on Enterprise Data / Master Data Management type solutions. She has developed requirements for several MDM initiatives, across various domains, within multiple organizations, working with different consulting companies, built on a variety of MDM software systems. The last MDM project she worked on was a completely new MDM initiative, in a domain where there was very little structured information available. Clear and concise requirements were essential to ensure that multiple concurrent development efforts could proceed efficiently after Solution Scoping.

While the majority of her time has been spent working on MDM solutions, she also has experience developing requirements for other types of systems including:

- *Data Warehouse systems*
- *Front End Application systems*
- *Core Processing systems*
- *Transaction Processing systems*

She developed this guide to share with other requirements analysts the approach she uses to gather, document, and manage requirements for a Master Data Management solution. This approach has evolved over time, incorporating lessons learned from prior experiences.

Suggested Reading - Books

The following are suggested reading for additional information on Master Data Management, Requirements Techniques, Data Modeling, or Data Management:

- DAMA International, *The DAMA Guide to the Data Management Body of Knowledge (DAMA-DMBOK)*, Technics Publications, LLC, 2009
- Dreibelbis, Allen, Eberhard Hechler, Ivan Milman, Martin Oberhofer, Paul van Run, Dan Wolfson, *Enterprise Master Data Management, An SOA Approach to Managing Core Information*, IBM Press, 2008
- Hoberman, Steve, *Data Modeling Made Simple – A Practical Guide for Business and IT Professionals, 2nd Edition*, Technics Publications, LLC, 2009
- IIBA - International Institute of Business Analysis, *BABOK Guide - A Guide to the Business Analysis Body of Knowledge, Version 3.0*, 2015
- IIBA - International Institute of Business Analysis, *Agile Extension to the BABOK Guide, Version 1.0*, 2013
- Loshin David, *Master Data Management*, Morgan Kaufmann, 2009

Made in the USA
Coppell, TX
16 March 2022

75076050R00031